Carrier's Cart to Oxford

Mildred Masheder MA, Ac.Dip.Ed is a former primary teacher and senior lecturer in child development and multi-cultural studies at the University of London. She has subsequently held research fellowships exploring peaceful conflict resolution and cooperation with young children, and is the author of a number of books – including *Let's Cooperate, Let's Play Together, Let's Enjoy Nature, Windows to Nature, Freedom from Bullying*, the play section of *Natural Childhood*, and most recently *Positive Childhood: Educating Young Citizens*. She has also produced a video on cooperative play and parachute games.
Mildred Masheder has two daughters and two grandchildren.

Carrier's Cart to Oxford

Growing up in the 1920s in the Oxfordshire Village of Elsfield

Mildred Masheder

Illustrations by Susanna Masheder

THE WYCHWOOD PRESS

First published in 2007 by
The Wychwood Press

an imprint of Jon Carpenter Publishing
Alder House, Market Street, Charlbury, Oxfordshire OX7 3PH
☎ 01608 811969

ISBN 978-1-902279-28-2

Manufactured in England by LPPS Ltd, Wellingborough NN18 3PJ

Contents

The author as a toddler

This book is dedicated to my father and my
mother and my brother, Monty.

Acknowledgments

I would like to give my heartfelt thanks:

to Susanna Masheder for her tireless work in researching the archives for the photographs; also for her drawings of country life;

to Guadalupe G. de Turner for her invaluable support in preparing and editing the manuscript and taking the photographs;

to Bessie Phipps, Did and Agnes Aarner, Betty Webb and Jimmy Maltby for gladly sharing their recollections of our childhood in the village;

to the Oxfordshire Photographic Archive for the reproduction of early photographs.

Foreword

I am delighted to commend *Carrier's Cart to Oxford* as an absolutely fascinating, absorbing social history of village life in the 1920s. Mildred Masheder's picturesque account of a child growing up in the small village of Elsfield, near Oxford, gives life to a well-crafted picture of a bygone age. There is so much to learn and to enjoy on each page of this brilliantly written book. For instance, we learn about life in the busy home, the disciplined village school and the labour intensive farm. We explore an almost forgotten vocabulary (ruched bonnets) as Mildred takes us on a unique journey as she revisits the distant scenes of English rural life.

We are given sensitive insights into the psychological and social development – hopes and fears – of a child growing up in the village. The earthy customs, sometimes brutal (killing the family's pig) are so described that the reader is able to feel a part of the drama. I believe that this delightful history may be favourably compared with well-known works such as *Lark Rise to Candleford* and *Cider with Rosie*. A range of readers, including pupils researching the social history of the 19th century, will appreciate it and gain much from its pages. I am sure it will be essential reading for budding historians and a welcome addition in school and college libraries.

I believe what makes Mildred's account so relevant for the modern reader is the way that she implicitly invites us to contrast and compare the values of life (principles that guide behaviour) as we now experience them, with those of our forebears living in the 1920s. For instance, what impressed me, as I suspect it will others, was the strict, predictable order that governed home and village life reflecting values such as care, responsibility and respect.

'We took for granted the steady routine that permeated all of our lives and just as we were actively conscious of the cycle of the seasons, so we were equally aware that the regular order of our home life was every bit as constant.'

The rhythm of a country life, which was still so bound to the natural cycle of farming, is in stark contrast to life experienced today in Elsfield, which we are told is, 'now a ghost of its former vibrating spirit'. Sadly now, the village is comprised of a preponderance of middle class residents (no doubt daily commuters) with the remaining farm workers as inhabitants of old folk's homes. The value system of the village in the 1920s stood firm on the twin pillars of a traditional structure of family life and a stable, well-ordered local community. The extreme individualism, which we experience in the 21st century, could have no place at a time that still needed the active cooperation of a large manual workforce to ensure economic success. The village stands out as an interdependent supportive network inviting us to consider the way we lead our lives today.

Mildred Masheder's *Carrier's Cart to Oxford* is a joy to read and on finishing it I could not wait to get in my car and visit Elsfield as it is today: more importantly, to stand near the site of the old village school and relive in my imagination the scenes she so poetically described. I invite you to enjoy your journey through the following pages too…

Dr. Neil Hawkes
International Values Consultant
Former Senior Education Adviser for Oxfordshire
Oxford

Chapter 1

Home

My earliest recollection is of the anticipation of going to Liverpool when I was almost three years old. There were great preparations and hustle and bustle, as it was the first time anyone in the family had had a holiday, and this was only for me and my mother, leaving my brother aged 6 and my father to look after the farm and there was 'Aunt Gert' to look after them; she wasn't a real aunt, but what was called a mother's help.

As the time drew near for Mr. Gatz's car from Beckley to take us to the station, I was lifted onto my father's heavy writing desk to watch for the car to arrive along the Stowood road. My mother impressed me with the fact that it was very important to know when he was coming and I felt that it all depended upon me to alert them. I realised later that this was just a ploy to stop a three-year-old from being under their feet during the flurry of last minute instructions.

The watching and waiting was an eternity. I kept to my post stolidly like a soldier on guard, my nose pressed firmly against the implacable window. I was aware of the weight of responsibility, probably for the first time in my short life. I protested loudly and voraciously when they tried to convince me that no car was coming from Beckley and that the train for Liverpool had already steamed out of Oxford station. I clung to my post, clutching at my fine straw hat stitched with tiny roses as they tried to remove it. The boy, who had been sent across the fields to find out what had happened, finally came back breathless, saying that Mr. Gatz had thought it was the following day. Another wait for eternity! It left me with a permanent sense of loss when plans did not materialise. Once when I went to the airport to go the United States and was told, "Come back tomorrow," as my visa was in my old passport, which I had omitted to bring, my heart sank just as it did when I was made to realise that keeping my hat on would not make everything alright.

My Parents

I know that I am a perfect Freudian case and I can only plead mitigating circumstances: namely that just at the time of my birth my mother caught the dreaded Spanish flu, so it was decided that I must be weaned straight away and put into the arms of my father, who did all the caring things that a good father can do. This bonding lasted all my life and was greatly consolidated by my consuming passion for the great outdoors, which was the men's world, whereas any household duties were always a chore. My memories of my mother are somewhat blurred and distant. Looking back I see how she toiled all day long from the time she brought up our hot water to reading to us before bed. On the other hand, memories of my father are vivid and clothed with emotion. Later I realised how my preference must have hurt her profoundly and I tried to make up for it.

My Father

My father was probably the person who had the biggest influence on me throughout my life. I had never really bonded with my mother in the same way. So it fell to my father to sing me to sleep and, long before I had any memory of this, I still know which songs they were, as when I hear them teardrops form in my eyes. There were sentimental songs from the first world war, which was still raging, and even one of earlier wars about a pensioner who gets his chair put by the window to see 'the queen, the queen go by'. This was of course Queen Victoria and the song was full of sentimentality and patriotic pride.

Apart from the first world war songs: 'Tipperary', 'Keep the home fires burning' and 'Pack up your troubles', my father had a wide repertoire from the music halls, which were popular in Oxford when he was growing up. My favourite was the 'Merry Widow', the valse, with the words, 'I'm going down to Maxims and you can go to…' and, instead of the swearword, 'hell', he would snap his fingers which I tried to imitate without success. I thought Maxims must be the zenith of depravity, and judged it in my limited vision, a naughty place and I was disappointed years later when I went to taste of its delights to find that it was a most expensive restaurant and that I couldn't afford it. Another song was 'Take a pair of sparkling eyes' from Gilbert and Sullivan's 'Gondoliers', when he would look down at me with his crystal-clear, blue eyes as though it was my eyes that were sparkling as they reflected in his. The family was enchanted with the whole repertoire of Gilbert and Sullivan and went year after year to the performances at Oxford and mother played the songs on Sunday nights when we sang round the piano, so that I still know most of the witty words by heart, although I no longer feel anything of my previous attachment to them, except those my father imprinted in my heart.

Father would always comply with my demands if I was ill in bed, which happened quite frequently as I was a chesty child. He would bring his shaving tackle into my bedroom and I would watch with great intensity while he sharpened his 'cut-throat' razor on a wide leather strap and then proceeded to lather and scrape his face until he was 'as smooth as a baby's bottom' as he would put it. He would pretend to chase me with his badger shaving brush full of lather when I wasn't safe in bed and I would run away screaming with excitement. There was also the thrill of another chase: before he shaved he would pursue me with the threat of "I'll scrub you!" But, when caught, I was given the merest touch of the bristles. Today, would these frolics be misinterpreted?

We would always go for a walk on Sunday evenings in the summer, even further than beyond our own (rented) fields. This unknown territory was cloaked in mystery for me and, whenever I hear the ringdoves coo, I recall those magical twilights in the heart of Long Wood, with my father carrying me on the last homeward stretch. It was on one of these occasions that I had the realisation of the close relationship between love and hatred. It was bound to come, but I was in no way prepared for it: the day when I was too big to be carried uphill back home. I was consumed with anger at him and his quiet explanation as to why he couldn't carry me cut no ice. Fortunately this explosion of my feelings did not last: he was still the one who never forgot the Mackintosh's Assorted Toffees after market on Wednesday; he knew that my first favourite was treacle and the second peppermint and never once did the assortment not contain one of each of them.

My Mother

If my mother had been born a generation later she would probably have continued as a dedicated teacher and would have made her mark in educating future teachers. She accepted her lot as a full time farmer's wife as being in the natural order of things and I can register my gratitude for her unceasing devotion in keeping the home going and giving the family a sense of well-being and security.

Her greatest joy was in participating in the village social life: playing the popular tunes at the village dances, the church organ for services, holding the position as trea-

Me on a pony, with my mother.

surer of the Women's Institute, 'the keeper of our purse' as Mrs. Buchan described her, ardent member of the Mothers' Union and, most important of all, the star actress in the drama group. These occasions might only have been once a month, but for her it was something to live for and express herself. When we finally had to move farms and she found herself completely isolated from the warm relationships with everyone in the village in a lone farmhouse, a mile from a tiny hamlet, she fell into a deep depression which took years to clear.

My Brother Monty

Although we grew up together and had all of our meals together, it was as if we were two only children for the amount of communication we shared. I think that we both accepted this as being quite normal: he indulged in boys' pursuits, but I was gradually conspiring to enter the man's world after finally relinquishing my dolls and playing 'houses' with the other village girls. Monty seemed quite self-sufficient in exploring the countryside far and wide with his constant companion, Perp Newell, who was a hunchback. I only had a vague idea of what they got up to: bird's nesting was, I am sure, their favourite and this resulted in beautiful collections arranged in old chocolate boxes full of sawdust. Being three and a half years older than me, it was understandable that I was not in their orbit.

I have to admit that I was quite jealous of Monty's relationship with my mother. It was epitomised by her constant recollection (at least to me it seemed constant) of the time when, at two years old, Monty nearly died of pneumonia. The reminder of her grief was brought out from its perfumed box: a pair of fawn kid gloves apparently suitable for a two year old to wear with tiny fingers and thumbs. She would recount how she had said, on receiving them as a present, "He'll never wear them" and I would think, "Too true, how on earth could you get a two year old to get all the fingers and thumbs into the right slots?" But I had of course missed the point and it was only when I myself was a mother that I began to understand her need to go over a situation that could have turned out so badly. To his credit, I don't think Monty was aware of my jealousy and I'm sure that he did not reciprocate with regard to the closeness of my special relationship with my father. At last, now our parents are dead, our relationship is one of great warmth and care.

Our Pets

Our pets were always considered an integral part of the family. Although we always seemed to have seven cats and only one dog at a time, dogs were much higher up in our esteem than the cats. Each Jack Russell terrier we possessed was to bring out my deepest emotions of joy and sorrow: the sheer exuberance of chasing them round the fields and the grief at their untimely deaths.

Jack Russells were literally prized, as father had once won a prize at Crufts for his wire-haired fox terrier with 'a straight back and upright tail'; that was before my time, when he had more time to concern himself with its care and training. He always knew exactly what to do about dogs and was keen on encouraging us children to feed them properly and never overfeed them, always leaving them slightly hungry. He explained to us that the dog would eat some more if you gave it to him, but this was just enough for him to clear up and he would do better like that. His relatives at Garsington used to look after the beagles used for hunting hares and we continued the tradition in a more familial way.

The deaths of Tiny, Worry and Patch had a profound effect on me: it was my first intimation of the finality of life – a life so full of energy and enthusiasm. It was bad enough that Tiny had been shot by mistake for a rabbit by Mr. Hatt, the neighbouring farmer, when he was invited for a day's shoot; but when Worry was found drowned in the cesspool, I thought that that was the most horrible death one could have. But it was Patch's death that troubled me most, as, although he had been declared officially dead, I could see him in the courtyard from my bedroom window, twitching about like a puppet on a string and I was sure that he was still in agony. I wept bitterly.

The cats were less traumatic, although dearly loved; they were all quite independent and spent most of their time ratting and mousing round the farmyard. They had their hierarchies: Joyce, a tortoiseshell with a ripple of tabby, was clearly the matriarch. She produced Beauty, who was utterly true to her name: clear patches of snow white, orange and black with no trace of the mottled effect of tabby, which was disdained as ordinary. Tortoiseshells like Beauty are much less common nowadays owing to the relative shortage of ginger toms and the increase of tabbies, illustrated by Florrie who was half tortoiseshell and half tabby.

Why did we have so

many cats and why were they all female? We

had never heard of spaying, at least I hadn't, and the toms were always around and active in the village. I became aware that their litter was almost always seven and later my arithmetic was well able to calculate forty-nine, for our family alone, and as the litter was inevitably twice a year, that was getting on for a hundred per family.

We had an unwritten law that once their eyes were open the kittens could not be drowned, as was always their fate if discovered in time. Our cats would always burrow deep into the heart of the hayricks to have their babies and only bring them out when their blue, blue eyes were wide open, staring appealingly at us from a wealth of soft fur. How different from the writhing, naked bodies that were handed over to Mr. Higgs, the day man, to perish in a bucket.

I was always convinced that the cats knew how to work the system and that they were sure that we could never destroy their precious offspring once we had seen how beautiful they were. I know now that they are only taken out to walk with their mother when they are really old enough; but part of me still believes in the strategies of maternal cats. In any case no-one could even reach the litters through the tunnel in the heart of the ricks, not even a small child, who would inevitably be on the side of the cats. Somehow we always found homes for them in the village and they would earn their keep as good mousers and ratters.

The Daily Rhythm

We took for granted the steady routine that permeated all of our lives and just as we were actively conscious of the cycle of the seasons, so we were equally aware that the regular order of our home life was every bit as constant. Didn't everyone wake up to their mother carrying a jug of boiling water to be placed in the washbasin with a towel over it to keep it warm until we crawled out of bed? For most of the year getting up and dressing was decidedly chilly and this was the incentive to get down to breakfast with the range already warming the sitting room, again lit an hour earlier by my father.

We wriggled into our warm clothes after a speedy wash at the basin, including necks and behind the ears. In winter we always wore combinations, which covered most of our body down to the legs. When I went for an interview to Milham Ford School, the headmistress, who had eyes like a hawk, asked what was the matter with my legs. My mother explained, "It's her combinations." No! I was mortified. On top was a liberty bodice with suspenders to hoist up the thick black woollen stockings, woollen knickers, then jumper and skirt, topped with a little cotton apron and finally, a lace-up pair of black boots for all weathers. It is no wonder that some families were reputed to 'sew their children up for the winter', but, as far as I knew, not in our village. In summer we discarded the heavy gear for cotton and button-up shoes.

There was the same sense of security in the constancy of our meals. Our breakfast was always ready for us: porridge in the winter, with the circular patterns that we made with Lyons Golden Syrup. Our plate of fried egg and bacon was waiting on the range: eggs that we had collected the day before and thick slices of bacon from the pig that father had cured. In summer, porridge was replaced by cornflakes, which had just been introduced under the name of 'Force' and we followed the adventures of Mr. Force with fascination: he was a half-moon shaped man who had miraculous powers and as much strength as Popeye. The implication that we would become as strong as him if we ate his cornflakes was not lost on us.

We toiled back from school for our regular sequence of dinners. The rhythm was cold roast on Monday with bubble and squeak; mince on Tuesday with little triangles of toast; Shepherds' Pie on Wednesday; baked rabbit on Thursday with the 'piggy back' always reserved for me; fish from the fish man on Friday; sausages on Saturday and of course the roast on Sunday. We never seemed to tire of this regime and, although we did not know the word organic, the accompanying vegetables were all from our garden, cultivated by my parents after a hard day's work.

Then there were the puddings, with a different favourite every day: roly poly, baked jam roll, queen of puddings, bread-and-butter pudding and, on Sundays, sherry trifle or summer pudding, all now being revived in expensive restaurants. We called it garden, rather than summer pudding, because we always went out to the garden to pick the redcurrants and yellow and red raspberries as the staple ingredients. Our favourite was sherry trifle and my mother would go to great lengths to ensure there was cream on it. She would creep out on Saturday nights to the dairy, armed with a shallow strainer and skim the cream from the top of the milk and then there would be cream on the Sunday trifle. My father would protest vehemently: if they analysed a sample of it and it was found to be fat-deficient, we would lose our livelihood. To my mother it seemed such a little drop to take from the ocean of milk and we children felt the same.

Tea was a gentler affair with thinly cut bread and butter, cut to the shape of the cottage loaf, homemade jam and various assortments of cakes. The staple cake was a solid fruitcake, which magically always lasted from one Sunday tea to the next when it was replenished with another identical one. To accompany it there was always a Victoria Sandwich, probably institutionalised by the queen herself. My mother then rang the changes to add to her repertoire: raspberry buns, rock cakes, Belgian almond slices, flapjacks – nothing fancy, but they all disappeared like hot cakes! In the summer we would cut a fresh lettuce, which tasted bitter to me. I think they went for size and so they were beginning to go to seed, just as enormous marrows and giant kidney beans took all the prizes at the flower and vegetable shows. This well-provided life-style was made possible by the untiring work of my parents and the mother's help. It was the same rhythm day after day, starting with lighting of the range until our bread and milk – hot milk – in winter and Eiffel Tower lemonade and biscuits in summer and, when we were ill, lemonade made with real lemons and fruit jellies. After eating a packet of yellow jelly when convalescing after bronchial pneumonia, I could never touch yellow jellies ever again.

House Work

Breakfast and midday dinner were always cooked and entailed a ritual of washing-up: a big bowl filled with hot water from the kettle was placed on the kitchen table together with our biggest tray for drainage. The soap-saver, full of the last pieces of our washing soap, was briskly whisked to produce a lather and, if I was not at school, I was commandeered to wipe up and put away.

The routine of stripping and airing the beds followed, with windows wide-open whatever the weather. In the interim the slops were collected in an enamel special bucket. I never knew where they were emptied, probably not in the privy, more likely on the garden, which might have enhanced our vegetables or might not.

Then the brass-railed beds were tackled with renewed vigour, with every double, feather mattress being turned and the layer of under blankets and sheets and their counter-parts duly smoothed out. Finally, the blankets and then the eiderdowns crowned the lot. It seemed a great palaver to me, roped in at weekends and holidays, especially as everything except the mattresses and eiderdowns had to be washed every week.

It was then time to start the midday dinner: first getting the produce from the garden, and in the summer that meant not only picking the peas and beans, but also podding and slicing them, not to mention the salads: lettuce and radishes for tea. In the winter there was always a store of potatoes, carrots, parsnips and turnips. The daily menu has already been described and it was always a credit to English home cooking, which has been unjustly derogated. There should have been a respite after the washing up, but that was the time that the chickens had to be fed with corn from the granary; I had forgotten to mention letting them out first thing and they all had a liberal interpretation of the freedom implied in the term 'free range', which of course we never used. Collecting the eggs was not my favourite job, but it was often assigned to me. You had to get the eggs from underneath setty hens, who would peck with deadly aim to defend their future offspring. Other eggs were out of doors and it would seem that the hens had a sixth sense to lay them in the most difficult places to find or to penetrate, like being hidden in the stinging nettles.

This was the cause of many providing a meal for the fox: an untimely death to those who wandered too far afield or who failed to clock in at bedtime. In spring, the women's job was to turn the eggs night and day in the large incubators until the chicks emerged in three weeks.

Teatime soon came round with the task of cutting paper thin bread and butter, with the two kinds of homemade jam and at least two kinds of cakes, all to be made and baked on 'free' afternoons. Evenings in the spring, summer and autumn were usually spent working in the garden when it was fine enough.

I have not mentioned the many other weekly tasks that were fitted into this timetable: the washing by hand, wringing out and hanging on the line and the ironing on the kitchen table with a flat iron; cleaning of the knives with corks and a special brown dust as they were not stainless; filling the oil lamps and trimming the wicks; washing the floors and carpet cleaning, dusting and polishing the heavy mahogany furniture, which had lots of intricate carving – I know, because that was one of my Saturday morning jobs.

The Privy

Only the better off farmers, the vicarage and the Manor had indoor toilets; the rest of us had a long walk down the garden and, when I was little, it seemed a much longer stretch than the 30 yards I estimated on an adult visit. There was a narrow path on the side of the garden, which was separated from the cow yard by a brick wall. In the autumn, the rampant Michaelmas daisies invaded the pathway and we were showered on going there and back; and as there was no immediate possibility of, "Now wash your hands!" this was often the alternative.

The privy was a broad wooden affair with an oval shaped carved hole with an ample supply of the Daily Mail torn into small sheets. When it was chock-a-block, the farm men had the unenviable task of emptying it all into a dung cart (how I never discovered) and depositing it in the cesspit halfway down the Little Field. This was where our beloved Jack Russell, Worry, got drowned. All the villagers had similar contrivances – some had extra little oval holes for children, which I envied. Of course this was only used for what we always called 'Pup' (I don't know how it would be spelt) and we never used the word 'shit'. The slops that were emptied every morning were a mixture of pee, collected from the po, and washing water and this was a good reason for opening all the windows to let the fresh air in. There were cleverly disguised commodes, like a pair of steps, for emergencies and, for the long winter evenings, there was a bucket in the scullery rather than make the hazardous journey to the bedroom with a candle. When we were ill, my mother would burn dried sprays of lavender to freshen the room and she would pace solemnly up and down the bedroom like a priestess. All of this procedure was so much part of our everyday lives and accepted as normal. Now, in another era, I frequently feel grateful for modern plumbing.

Candles and Lamps

I never experienced the benefits of electricity until I was eighteen and I still appreciate the comfort in switching on the light. Although I was not really afraid of the dark, I didn't much like going upstairs at night. We would sit by this lovely log fire all evening and then, when it came to going to bed, we would have to go up the stairs into this icy cold room and take all our clothes off and get into our nightgowns. We always had a candle and for years I thought, "Good night, mind the fat" was some kind of a blessing. The warning was not always heeded and I would take delight in wrestling pieces of hot fat from near the flame and then fashioning them into little animals – a foretaste of later work in ceramics with models of tigers and horses.

It's no wonder that our parents had to be especially vigilant: when the candle was blown out there was no bedside lamp to switch on. Monty was a regular sleepwalker and perhaps I tried to emulate him and managed it once, waking up to find I was standing on the bed but unable to move an inch. My parents came rushing up on hearing my screams and I got a lot of attention, but that was the only time: I think my body felt that it wasn't worth it. There was one occasion when I really became afraid of the dark. Monty had produced a thriller entitled, 'You'll Need a Night Light'. Mother forbade me to read it, but I got hold of it and I did need a night light! It was about a severed hand that came hurtling across the floor to cling to one's ankles. For months I did a running jump to leap into bed!

When did I give up kneeling at the foot of the bed, cold in my nightdress and with bare feet? Was it at this moment? I certainly wouldn't have dared risk the 'hand' grasping my ankles. I still recall the words, "Almighty God, I beseech thee to forgive for Christ's sake what Thou hast seen wrong in me today. Wash away my sins with the precious blood of Thy redeemer, that I may go to sleep in peace" and I did. If I had allowed myself to ponder over the words, I would certainly queried the propensity of blood being a good cleanser, but it was in the nature of a mantra and I was learning not to question all that was laid before me.

But there were real dangers in having lamps and candles: that of fire. On one occasion, Monty and I were sitting at the table when the heavy table lamp tilted and would have crashed onto the tablecloth on which the lamp was precariously balanced, breaking the glass bowl, which contained the oil. Monty had the presence of mind to spring up to steady it and was greatly praised by our parents, who rushed in from the kitchen. I was somehow made to feel that it was my fault, although I was unaware of having pulled the heavy tablecloth on which the lamp was standing.

It was not until I went to stay with Auntie Edie in Oxford that I experienced the blessings of electricity and I was overcome with wonder at the dazzling light at the turn of a switch; I still am sometimes!

I have gone into detail as a tribute to the women who worked long hours and got their reward from our appreciation of what was provided for us, which I'm afraid I took very much for granted. I should add that my father worked equally hard on the farm and made sure we were never short of logs for the fires. The only respite my parents seemed to have was on Sunday afternoons. After the special celebration of Sunday dinner and before the farmhouse tea, they had a well-earned rest in bed. Only once did I burst in on them and was completely taken aback by the frosty reception I received. I went away feeling isolated and rejected.

There was plenty of time for reading in those long winter evenings and I devoured all the books we had, which were mostly classics, over and over again. 'Alice in Wonderland' and 'Through the Looking Glass' I knew by heart. I recall once, when I was ill in bed with bronchitis, the Buchans sent a wonderful pyramid of books for me to read, with a huge one at the bottom and then gradually mounting to a tiny one at the top. This gesture made me feel that it was worth having bronchitis to be able to nestle down in bed with all of those treasured books. As soon as I was able to cycle to Oxford, I made straight for the junior library and enveloped myself in a host of girls' school stories, inspired by my weekly dose of 'School Friend', the girls' version of 'Billy Bunter'. Mother read to us every night, so I knew plenty of boys' adventure stories. She knew that I could appreciate yarns like 'The Three Midshipmen' and 'The Gorilla Hunters', but Monty couldn't have stomached Angela Brazil's adventurous accounts of life at a girls' boarding school. I always sympathised with the youngest, like Peterkin in 'The Three Midshipmen'.

Later we had our first wireless, a crystal set that had a 'cat's whisker' which you had to manipulate until you finally got some sound. I only seemed to manage to receive the endless sound of the sea, but I don't think that was the real programme. It was some time before we had a wireless that worked and even then I had to get right up close to it to get the dance tunes, precursors of pop, from Radio Luxemburg. The wireless did not interfere with our regular pursuits; at that stage it provided a background of music with a bit of news thrown in.

Country Tales

For me, the best entertainment of all was when my father told us stories and these were not confined to the winter evenings; he became especially inspired when any visitors came to the house and they enjoyed them as much as he did. There were neighbouring farming people who came to tea and also often buyers for a calf or dealers in corn (our word for oats, wheat and barley) and I would make a point of sitting in on these negotiations for two reasons. One was that when there was a final discrepancy in the bargaining, they would frequently say, "Give the difference to the little girl." It wasn't much, perhaps half a crown, but I was delighted with it and put it ostentatiously in my home safe. The other reason for my presence was that, business finished, they would happily listen to his wide repertoire of stories over a glass of beer and I would join in the peels of laughter, which was catching, especially when the tears rolled down father's cheeks as he rocked from side to side with sheer mirth.

Some of my Father's Favourite Tales

Some of the tales that my father told with such gusto were of incidents that I can only dimly recall. There was the time when the farm cat, a shaggy ginger tom, stole the cowman's milk, left for him in the dairy. Old Tom Dennis, the cowman, who had a nasty temper, shouted, "I'll have my bloody revenge on you!" My father, out of consideration for our innocent minds, said, "My b… revenge." Tom took a long piece of string, tied it around the struggling cat's neck and attached the other end to the gate. He fetched his airgun and aimed. Bang! The slug cut straight through the string and away went the cat like a bullet! My father at this stage would be convulsed with laughter, as his own relationship with his cowman would relish such a dishonourable incident.

Then there were shorter anecdotes, which I only understood later, although I always joined in the uproarious laughter. There was the old man who came to our house and was struck by the inscription 'Tempus Fugit' (Time Flies) on our clock. "Did ol' Tim Fuggit make your clock too? He made our'n!" Everyone had the title of 'old' as a sign of belonging and families

Bessie Phipps (right) and me sitting on the gate near our house.

always used the prefix 'our' in the sense of real possession. So it was always 'our mam', 'our dad', 'our Mont' and 'our Mil'.

Some of the tales stuck to people for the rest of their lives and after, especially if they had transgressed the accepted codes of behaviour, such as certain patterns of mutual help. One of these was the age-old tradition of the man bringing his wife a cup of tea in bed before she got up to tackle the hard day's work. There was an apocryphal story about 'bed tea' from the next village, where an old man and his wife hated each other. He would get up early every morning and lay the fire in the kitchen grate – newspaper, twigs and finely chopped wood – and then light a real 'blizzy' to get the kettle to boil. After his hot cup of tea, he would go out to the pump, draw a bucket full of water and slosh it all over the red-hot embers for when she got up! When she died, he died too; his raison d'être seemed to have departed with her.

There were few tales about politics, as we were mostly unaware of what our representatives were doing for us, and there was only a slight stir at election times, mostly concerned with whether to go all the way to Islip – four miles – to vote. The for and against were in fine balance, as the story of Mr. and Mrs. Tompkins shows. They were in their pony trap, just before they were going to negotiate Islip hill on a dark stormy night. Mr. Tompkins said to his wife, "Who be you going to vote for then?" She replied, "Well, I thought that young liberal man was very nice." "Whoa!" shouted Mr. Tompkins, "Back we go. I was going to vote Conservative, so we'd cancel each other out."

Ghost stories were always part of the repertoire. There was one about Tom, who always came back from the pub on a Saturday night very full of beer. This must have been in my father's youth at Garsington, as Tom had to walk through the churchyard on his way home. One night, the young men decided to play a trick on him when there was an open grave ready dug for the funeral. One of them lay in the grave and, as Tom went past, moaned and groaned calling out, "I can't rest. I can't rest." Tom rose magnificently to the occasion, swaying precariously over the open grave, "Of course you can't, you poor bugger, you bain't but half covered up!" Whereupon he set to shovelling the surrounding earth on top of the 'ghost' with such gusto that the moans and groans were instantly silenced. We children always wanted to know what happened next, but my father always said, "Ah, that's the end of the story."

Another one I liked was the one about "Old Turp Merrit" from Cowley, who was also in his cups when he got lost in Bagley Woods. He kept calling, "Lost, lost," and the owls replied, "Oo oo." His reply was "Old Turp Merritt from Cowley." But the response was always the same, "Oo oo." Finally he shouts, "Old Turp Merritt from Cowley, you bloody fool, can't 'e 'ear me?" The reply was of course, "Oo oo!" Later I read a similar story in Thomas Hardy's 'Under the Greenwood Tree'. My father didn't know of it, but he knew Old Turp Merritt and was sure it was true. So folk history merges with the living experience.

Other villages had their long-standing ghost stories. An uncle from Oddington never missed an opportunity to recount the 'true' story of the ghost of a woman, whose voice could be heard singing plaintively across the waters in the darkness of the night and although the melancholy voice seemed to come from the church tower, no-one had ever seen her. It was said that she was mourning for her faithless lover, who had deserted her in her hour of need, and that she had drowned herself rather than face the condemnation of the village. I would listen open-mouthed and believed every word of it, but I couldn't understand for the life of me why the village would have condemned her. I thought that they would have been sympathetic towards her and condemned the lover who had abandoned her, but when I raised this point of view, there were only meaningful looks and these somehow silenced me.

At Elsfield, our experiences were much less dramatic. There was Bessie Phipps who was doing the washing up where the corpse of Mrs. Brown was laid out in the next room. Suddenly, to her terror, the glasses started to move as they were put on the washboard and she thought it was ghosts, but in fact it was the water on the sloping board that caused them to move around!

Play in the Wide Open Spaces

We made our own fun and entertainment, both in our play and what the village provided for us, and whenever we could we were roaming the fields and woods feeling free as the wind. The grown-ups knew we would be safe and so they never worried, although they might have done if they had suspected the various escapades we got up to.

Our childhood was always governed by the seasons, each one having special attractions.

Spring was heralded with great bunches of primroses and bluebells, violets, anemones, cowslips and large oxlips.

But nothing could be quite as exciting as the summer: haymaking and harvest with endless bumpy rides in the wagons, going down to the hay and cornfields. Before they were cut, these lush meadows were redolent with early purple orchids, blue butchers, scabious and moon daisies and, later, bright red poppies and scarlet pimpernels in the cornfields. There was no restriction on picking them and we made beautiful bouquets and daisy chains and poppy ladies.

Autumn brought fruit in abundance: blackberries to make jam, the most delicious wild mushrooms, well matured by the carthorses' dung, and nuts galore. We went nutting, looking for sixers and even seveners.

In winter, we could generally find some holly with berries and once, on Christmas Day, we even found primroses on a sheltered bank. Even in the depths of winter our main delight was to go out to play, especially if there was a hard frost for sliding or a fall of snow, which seemed to be more frequent then. Just as the summer days seemed longer and hotter, so snow and ice were imprinted on our memories of the winter season. The moment the snow started falling, we couldn't wait to go out and play with it. Mother always said, "You'll be back crying with the cold" and when we were very young this was all too true. When we were a little older, we would make great snowballs, as well as snowmen, and rolled them down any grassy slope, so that by the time they had reached the bottom they had increased their bulk many times over, leaving a path of grass in their wake. Tin trays, which were a part of every household, were our toboggans. They skimmed the surface of the snow much better than the 'boughten' ones. This was one pejorative term for any food not home-made. When the catkins, pussy willows and the sticky buds came out again, we knew that it would be soon time to go out to play after tea and we would rush out to join the village kids for our favourite game of hide-and-seek, until the twilight covered the farm buildings with darkening shadows.

Our version of hide-and-seek was 'fox and hounds': there were usually several foxes and the rest were hounds. The foxes were given a set time to hide and then the rest of the pack would rush out, calling "Holler, holler, else the dogs won't foller!" and the foxes, crouched in the haystacks or under the ricks or hiding in the farm buildings, would have to 'holler', otherwise they risked being abandoned in the search. When we played it in the dusky twilight, with the moon just rising, there was always that frisson of danger when you were hiding in the dark recesses of the stables and cowsheds and we foxes would huddle together for comfort, as every shadow seemed to hide somebody who would jump out at us, to the point when we were actually relieved to be caught and to be reassured that it was only one of the hounds. It was equally scary when, as seekers, you were plunging into the huge pile of hay stacked in the barn, hoping yet dreading to find a body. I learnt much later that some of the older boys and girls took advantage of the darkness of the barns and the softness of the hay and didn't want to 'holler' and it took their mothers' anxious calls to lure them from their 'lairs'. These early explorations passed me by and, by the time I was their age, I was going to Oxford to the grammar school, which cut short any precocious adolescent explorations.

There were many other outdoor games, but this one appealed the most, although playing houses and farms was also the favourite in younger years, at least for the girls. The boys were always keen on exploring further afield, especially in bird nesting time and autumn scrumping.

In the long winter evenings when we could no longer roam the fields, card games were a regular family pastime, sitting round the table with the log fire blazing away. I enjoyed 'Strip Jack Naked', 'Beggar my Neighbour', 'Sevens Down the Middle' and 'Rummy'. As I was often on my own, 'Clock Patience' was my favourite, the last king being turned up spelt death to the game and, even in my young mind, it was associated with the hope of going on living until death caught up with you.

As soon as I was old enough and even before, I was commandeered to make up a four for whist and later bridge. For some time, all that was required of me was to hold up the cards and be the 'dummy'. This role was not to my taste, as I found it excessively boring and I felt that 'dummy' was a really diminishing term. However, I soon learnt to play quite a passable game, although I never wanted to continue to play cards in adult life. We sometimes would play for hazel nuts and when the shooting parties came they would play for low stakes and possibly the whole experience cured me of any latent gambling tendencies.

The other social activity was singing round the piano on a Sunday evening. We had all of Gilbert and Sullivan, lots of folk songs and a book of Sea Shanties. I loved 'Shenandoah' and sang lustily the refrain, 'Away I'm bound to go, Cross the wide Missouri' already thinking nostalgically of a future that would take me far away from Elsfield. I didn't realise then the immense value of living so close to Nature, although I took full advantage of its pleasures.

Our Relatives

We had relatives in abundance. Most of them were sited in or around Oxford, so there was intermittent contact in spite of limited transport. Our close relatives always considered themselves as part of the family, as did also some of the ones who were not so close.

The one standing commitment with relatives was to spend Christmas Day with Granny and Grandpa, together with all the uncles and aunts and cousins. I was always reluctant to leave the treasures and toys found in my stocking, but I had no choice. Our one extravagance was to go by Mr Gatz's taxi and I thought that this time he couldn't mistake the day.

On one occasion, we spent the whole of Christmas day rehearsing a knock-about, invented play with the cousins. I was full of apprehension and excitement at the idea of performing in public, but our plans were dashed to the ground when Granny decided that there was no time for our play. I was indignant – why did the grown-ups always decide? But I couldn't protest. I couldn't help thinking that there had been lots of time for my aunt to sing a whole series of Christopher Robin songs: 'Hush, hush, whisper who dares, Christopher Robin is saying his prayers' and 'Half way up the stairs is the stair where I sit. There isn't any other stair quite like it' and many more, which I considered rather sloppy.

I once stayed the night with them when I was old enough. I couldn't sleep because of the traffic and, when I finally got up, the rest of the household was still firmly asleep. There was no fire, only the ashes of the night before, and no breakfast. I couldn't wait to be fetched home to the country. An overnight stay with an aunt and uncle made me feel equally homesick, especially when I suffered the indignity of having my face briskly washed, together with my younger twin cousins. I might be a country 'bumpkin', but I had always washed myself.

The most cherished relatives of all were my mother's sister, Auntie Glad, with her husband, Uncle Jim, and cousin Beryl. When they came to stay, it was the fatted calf – in our case the home-cured ham. I'm afraid I couldn't help being jealous of Beryl: my father made such a fuss of her calling her 'Brumijum', which always made her laugh. One of the few times Monty and

I formed an alliance was when Beryl was put to bed in the dark cold room, my room in fact, as Monty and I had had to join up in his room. When she started calling for her mother, we listened with glee, at least I did. Auntie Glad's reply was, "What is it Beryl?" The response finally came, "I want to do my tiny wee drops!" Monty and I were convulsed with ill-disguised laughter. When they went back to Nuneaton, my mother always shed genuine tears and I tried to look sorrowful. Later Beryl and I became close friends, which has lasted until this day.

A lot has been written about the loss of the extended family in recent years and I am sure that this was a great support in the past and was certainly so with many of the villagers, especially the young couples. For us, the idealistic myth of the jolly farmer did have its shortcomings, but my mother's tears at their departure were genuine enough, in contrast to my ill-disguised relief.

There were more distant relatives living in London, second or third cousins, and they seemed always to invite themselves when the haymaking season was at its height. This put considerable strain on my parents, who were imbued with the farming code of hospitality, and they were sometimes stretched to the limits of their welcome, by such remarks as to how restful and relaxing the country was after London, while everyone else was trying desperately to get the hay carried in, before the rain soaked it all.

Our farm was a place where distant relations could always stay and this was the case with Cousin Carrie. Cousin Carrie had been the housekeeper to a widower who had two or three children and finally married her. At any mention of sex she said, "I don't know much about that sort of thing," so there wasn't much love in it. Later, when she herself was a widow and the war broke out, she was so terrified on the first day of war, when they tried out the sirens against air-raids in London, that she took a taxi, almost unheard of in our family, from Wandsworth right to our little village of Chiselhampton, where we had moved to before the war. She stayed for the duration, regaling us with awesome stories of how London was catching it, and of her own narrow escape by taxi. I don't know if she ever heard a bomb fall, but her descriptions of the terror were realistic enough and her favourite remark to us country people was, "Ah, but you haven't been through it!"

Harry Warren was a second cousin who lived in the East End of London and used to come to visit my grandparents in Oxford and soon betook himself to the farm, where he enjoyed the company of the boys. Although I tried desperately to endear myself to him, so that I too might get that coveted invitation to London, he never took the slightest notice of me. The grown-ups used to say, "How good Harry is with the children" and I knew that they had no idea what the attraction was and nor did I. For me, and I think my brother and our cousin Basil, it was the magic city of London that enticed us, where Dick Whittington had turned again to and where there had been a terrible fire. When the boys did go to the magic city, it was beyond their wildest dreams, but I was never invited.

Harry Warren was a confirmed bachelor, living with his sister, whom we called cousin Cud – why Cud? Today Harry might have been suspected of having a ulterior motives for inviting boys to stay with him, but whatever may have been latent, I am sure that such thoughts never entered his conscious mind. It was natural to have bachelors – in fact they were unwittingly called 'gay' – as it was to have spinsters, although the former were regarded as having escaped the clutches of women, whereas the latter were pitied and often looked down on.

Rabbiting

The only occasions when my family entertained, other than when relatives came to stay, were the days when uncles, my father's brothers, or Mr. Hatt, the farmer, would come for a one-day shoot, and occasionally Mr Wigmore, who owned the dairy where we sold our milk. To our amazement, he would bring his beautiful fair-haired daughter and she would shoot rabbits with the rest of them. Then we knew that it would be a wonderful 'tea-dinner' for us after school. My mother would make a roast, usually lamb, with all the trimmings and home-made redcurrant jelly, followed by trifle, the real sort with sherry, custard and cream, skimmed from the churns, waiting to go to the dairy in Oxford. It was always served on the best cobalt-blue dinner service and it tasted even better than Sunday lunch, with father officiating, with his usual leisurely sharpening of the carving knife, and my mother trying to hide her impatience, as all of her vegetables and gravy were getting cold. I was fascinated by his sheer dexterity and have never managed to get the same sleight of hand. It was

timed for 5 o'clock, when the shooters had returned, after storing their booty of rabbits in the tubs they had driven in.

The farm labourers, who had worked hard as 'beaters', banging sticks against sticks while advancing in a straight line, with the working terriers rounding up the rabbits caught in front of the onslaught, were rewarded with their share, which they hung on a stick slung across the handle-bars of their bikes.

Only once were our appetites diminished and that was when Johnny Bonnet, as we always called him behind his back, shot our little Jack Russell terrier, Tiny, in mistake for a rabbit. We thought, "How could he?" Tiny was pure white and the rabbits were brown; but he was so upset and contrite that we managed to forgive him. But that death was traumatic for me: it was my first encounter with the realisation that we were not immortal.

We children never participated in the shoots, even when we were older; perhaps my parents were afraid that we might suffer the same fate as Tiny. But for me, I would never have had a taste for such a so-called sport. But of course rabbiting was the privilege of the tenant farmers and rabbits formed a substantial part of our meat; the farm workers were supposed to pay 6d a rabbit, except when on duty 'beating', but they were often tempted to poach them and who could blame them. It was the lord of the Manor who had all the rights to the game, mostly pheasants and partridges, which we were not allowed to shoot.

But for me there was a downside to these social occasions. If Mr. Hatt stayed on to play cards, which made up a four, he would always say with a twinkle in his eye, "I'll play with Mildred." As he had a large bulbous pipe, which was drooping neglected as he breathed heavily over his choice of card, I felt that I had been encased in a cage of smoke, bound round by his massive great arms. The alternative was to be a sort of card stand, when I was really making up the four. Then he would whip round from his seat, when it was my turn to choose a card, to choose one for me and then back again in time to play his own hand.

There was an added problem for me when the uncles stayed late for cards until about eleven o'clock. This meant I had to kiss them before I went to bed. They both had drooping moustaches, although Uncle Bert's was kept in relatively better shape than Uncle Tubb's (he was always called 'Uncle Tubb', after he had once nicknamed my father, 'Barrel'). I felt that kissing Uncle Tubb was more like kissing a mop rather than a moustache: it tended to drip from the beer or whisky that he had been imbibing. I had the distinct impression that they enjoyed it far more than I did. I finally got to sleep after hearing them harnessing the ponies into the traps and lighting the oil lamps for the long drive to Oxford or Garsington.

Chapter 2

The Farm

We took for granted that the farm, its buildings and fields, were our domain, where we could wander freely and where no harm would come to us. Our parents were always busy and had no idea of what we were up to, and it was that trust that formed a precious bond between us. We knew that we were loved and cared for and at the same time we enjoyed independent lives, which they were not a part of.

If they had known about the risks we ran they would have been less tranquil, but somehow we made our own boundaries and only attempted what we knew we could achieve with a certain amount of courage and daring. For me, one escapade was to climb up the perpendicular ladder to the granary high up above the barn. This was no great feat in itself; it was my imagination of it coming unstuck and carrying me under it, crashing to the concrete floor below, that provided the drama. I was always relieved when I could swing my body round and alight on the granary floor. But the real test was to jump from the granary opening onto the wagon loaded with hay below. The frisson was in the fact that there was a three feet gap between the top of the hay and the jump-off spot with a 30 feet drop onto the concrete floor below. With a feeling of awe and anxiety, I would steel myself for the leap, aiming at the centre of the hay so that I wouldn't slither off on landing. I never did!

Other escapades included making little bonfires out of dried hay between the hayricks with a magnifying glass to capture the rays of the sun. We were blissfully unaware of the danger to the ricks and, fortunately for us, our father was in that same state of ignorance of what was going on, as it could have meant ruination if they had been burnt down. I would maintain that this was not vandalism – more like innocence, mixed with stupidity.

So we ran free – out into fields redolent with moon daisies, vetch, corn-cockles and the early purple orchids, which we called 'butcher boys'. Our wanderings led us to the river Cherwell where we would pick tall bulrushes and yellow iris and spot the electric blue of the kingfisher rising from the banks. There too we had guardian angels looking after us. When Emily Watts, a non-swimmer, got out of her depth and clung to me like a limpet in a

Sescut Farm on the banks of the River Cherwell, 1885. © Oxfordshire County Council
Photographic Archive.

complete state of panic, somehow the two of us managed to scramble to the
bank and I said to Emily, "We must pray to God to say thank you," although
at the time during the struggle, I don't think either of us had the presence of
mind to make any such request for salvation.

So what were the highlights of life on the farm for us? Apart from year-
round play in the buildings and woods, there were very special times like
haymaking and harvest. But for me, at a very early age, the biggest attraction
was the blacksmith's shop at the end of our long garden.

The Blacksmith's Smithy

From the age of three onwards, I was drawn, like a bee to a honey-pot, to
the smithy attached to the farmyard. The shed was at the end of our back
garden and I would creep over the fence surrounding our outside lavatory and
spend hours glued to the actions of Jack Nappin, the blacksmith. He had a
red face and an even redder bulbous nose and his pipe was always well established at the corner of his mouth. His leather apron had matured with
constant pressure against the horse's body and his cap shiny with a mixture
of grease and sweat.

As I watched his every movement, I was fully versed in the sequence of
events: first there was the gentle persuasion needed to get these huge

carthorses to raise one leg at a time and to be held firmly between his legs, gently it's true, but not without a string of swear words, to which I was completely oblivious. I knew instinctively that it was part of his magic. Then came the wrenching off of the old shoes, each nail being pulled out with an outsize pair of pincers. Then came the trimming of where the hoof had become overgrown; with deft turns of the scalpel, he shaped them back into a neat circle.

The whole process was a treat for all of my senses: the roar of the bellows, the stirring of blue flames into a seething glow of oranges and reds in the forge, with the new shoes almost white hot as the blowing increased. What I loved was the ring of the hammer on the red hot iron, with sparks flying in all directions, including mine, heavy blows followed by a few trills on the anvil itself, as if to steady the main thrust. Then came the crowning moment, when he carried the red hot shoes to the water trough and the sudden sizzle as he plunged them into the cold water, immersing me in a cloud of hazy steam. Even more breathtaking was when the tempered shoes were fitted and then a glorious aroma of burning hooves pervaded the whole shed with jets of thick blue smoke. That was the climax: the nails being hammered in and their ends wrenched off with enormous pliers finished the shoeing. But this had less appeal, as I found it hard to believe that it didn't hurt, although the horses gave no signs of distress.

During the whole of this performance I was perched quite near on a smooth, thick, oval-shaped pole, which was lodged precariously on the shelves that lined the walls. It was placed diagonally across a corner, so that there was just enough room for me to sit more or less suspended in mid-air. It seemed that there was an unspoken rapport between the blacksmith and me, as little, if any, verbal communication took place. It was understood that this was my place and I knew instinctively my part of the bargain was to keep balanced on the slippery oval-shaped pole, wedged between two soot-encrusted ledges. I soon discovered that if I tipped the least bit backward or forward it would do a quick somersault, which I knew would either send me into the heap of soot in the corner or, much worse, precipitate me dangerously near the glowing forge. In either case it might have disturbed the enormous carthorse, which he had managed to coax into submission, and that, I felt, would be the end of my tolerated visits. Generally however, he accepted my presence as part of the natural order of things.

There was another reason for sitting still: the shelves were lined with exciting looking tins extolling Mackintoshes' toffee, chocolate biscuits and sweets and, in my innocence, I always hoped that one day, if I was very good, I might be asked to partake of them. So I soon learned to sit as quiet as a mouse. The fact that there were plenty of jam jars, full of nails and the odd rusty horseshoe, did not alert me to the obvious content of the enticing tins.

To this day, I am still convinced that I could shoe a horse, perhaps as long as it wasn't a carthorse!

Haymaking

Haymaking might have been an overwhelmingly busy time for all of the farm workers and also for my parents, but for us children it was thrilling. We would take endless rides down the fields in the empty wagons, being bumped about all the way as the metal wheels went in and out of the deep furrows which had been eroded by heavy cartloads throughout the seasons. We sat on the slatted sides of the wagons, clutching the bars with both hands to keep ourselves from being flung on to the floor, and to us it had all the thrill of the big dipper (which we had never experienced but we could imagine).

For me, the crowning glory of haymaking was when I was allowed to take the reins to 'have a go' at side-raking. This was driving the carthorse up and down the rows of mown hay, so that the rotating metal rakes turned the hay to enable the underside to dry in the sun. I felt as exalted as a Roman charioteer, bouncing up and down on my swinging metal seat, framed more for a farm worker than an eight year old's skinny backside. I fondly imagined that I was controlling a mettlesome steed, but in fact I was always allocated old Flower, who knew exactly where she was going and was quite independent

Wagon for haymaking and harvest. We would sit precariously on the sides as the empty wagons went down to the fields.

My father swarth turning with Blackbird.

of my frantic efforts to make her play a more high-powered role and, if she sensed anything of my elation, it was with an indulgent tolerance. I gradually became proficient at turning at the end of the row without cutting corners, as Flower had a feeling that if she turned before the end of the field somehow she would be finished sooner – which was actually correct reasoning. I later progressed to horse rake, which was much more difficult as you had to judge just the right moment to lift the lever, which controlled the accumulation of the remnants of the hay and deposit it in a straight line. Mine was usually a zigzagged performance, which tried the patience of the men who were guiding the elevator to pick up the final rakings. However they tolerated my efforts just as they tolerated the wiles of my shaggy old pony, Dot.

Dot was always commandeered during haymaking and harvest to work the wheels that drove the elevator to carry the hay or corn sheaves from the wagons onto the ricks. This was achieved by harnessing her to a shaft that she was supposed to drive by going round and round in a circle. But Dot had other ideas, together with a wondrous sense of timing. She would proceed round and round while the men were climbing up the ladders to the rick or the hay cart; then at the moment when they were installed, she would stop dead and no amount of coaxing and shouting, "Come on Dot" would budge her. Finally one of them would scale down the ladder and at the exact moment when he reached the bottom rung, Dot would break into a sprightly canter as if by clockwork, which threatened to break the whole haymaking machine; and then, as soon as he reached the top again, the whole diabolical business would start all over again.

I felt somewhat responsible for this impasse, as I knew that the only

Above: Loading the hay by hand, 1925.
Below: Loading hay with the elevator, 1930.
© Oxfordshire County Council Photographic Archive.

possible solution was for someone to go round and round behind her; I also knew that all hands were pointing to me to do it. And so round and round I went, sometimes cadging a lift on the shaft; Dot immediately retaliating with an abrupt stoppage in protest against the extra pounds of my lithe body. With Dot it was a real question of 'we and they' and, in this situation, I too was part of the establishment that was exploiting her.

But there was always a welcome respite at meal times for horses, men and children alike. At midday there was always the hot meal in a basin provided by the womenfolk at home and tea was a picnic in the hay fields under the shade of the oak trees that grew in the hedgerows. Haymaking was always during the summer term and it was the custom to let anyone, who had to take the men's tea, off early from school. As always, boys were given preference for this important duty, possibly because their presence was not so welcome at school, but also because it was considered a male prerogative.

I recall one occasion when my brother had gone off triumphantly without me and I made the singing lesson so unbearable that the teacher finally admitted defeat, almost pushing me out of the circle with, "Oh, go on then!" I was probably growling in protest which upset the vigour of 'Men of Harlech', 'Wi' a Hundred Pipers', 'Hearts of Oak' and such like patriotic fervour. My exit was even more triumphant than Monty's; the boycott had been well worth it. We would go down the fields laden with old glass beer bottles, full of piping hot, sweet, milky tea, wrapped in wads of newspaper: our primitive thermos flasks and they certainly kept the heat. Thinly cut sandwiches, cut right across the cottage loaf, were oozing with homemade raspberry or blackcurrant jam, which gave them a red lining, and then every kind of cake: Victoria sandwich, raspberry buns, chocolate sponge and rich fruit cake. We carriers felt that we deserved as much as the menfolk, as the bottles of tea were quite a burden. We would settle down to eat our fill and then lie back in a bed of sweet smelling hay.

There was still one place in the village where the haymaking was carried out as in feudal days: that is with cutting it with reaping (ripping in the vernacular) hooks or large scythes and then raking it into heaps with great wooden forks. This was at the Buchans' Manor House, where there was no access for a horse-drawn machine. As there was only a small field below the garden, it was very different from the gruelling labour of the feudal times. Everyone lent a hand, including all of the chauffeur's family and the Buchan children, with much hilarious tossing and turning of the heavily scented hay with two-pronged forks.

Harvesting

We all agreed that harvesting wasn't a patch on haymaking, but some delights remained the same: riding down in the empty wagons, although the corn was more scratchy than the hay; and there were still the teas to take down, without the buzz of being excused the last lesson of school as it was always during the summer holidays. We enjoyed the magical services of a binder, which took in the cut corn and ejected it ready tied in bundles. These sheaves were stacked into shocks or stooks and we would play houses in them or pretend they were wigwams and we were 'Red Indians'. Cutting with reaping hooks was a hardship that we heard of from the older workers: the men slashed the corn down and the women followed tying them into bundles with string. But even with the binder, the pace was arduous, as the men had to catch each sheaf with a two-pronged fork and balance them into stooks.

One custom still remained: when the square of uncut corn was getting smaller and smaller, all of the wildlife, the field mice, voles and rabbits would take refuge there, until terrified as the last swathes were falling, they would make a hopeless dash for it, only to be hacked down by the men and boys who were well prepared with heavy sticks. The men had made sure that they had tied up their trousers with bag tie just below the knee, as the mice were known to take refuge up the trouser legs. The spectacle sickened me and I would run off so as not to hear the shrill cries of the animals and the bludgeoning noise as they were killed. For the men it was a sort of primitive sport, but also it provided them with a few good dinners.

A more peaceful tradition was still maintained: that of gleaning. This was the women's role and they would gather any ears of corn that had been left behind on the field to feed their chickens. The older women still wore the ruched bonnets, which came down over their necks at the back to protect them from the sun. When the hats were new they were probably white, but the heat of the sun and constant washing with the blue bag had given them an off-white slightly lavender shade. I was once landed with one, presumably

Oxfordshire harvest: the reaper cut the corn and the stooks were our wigwams. © Oxfordshire County Council Photographic Archive.

The 'old steam roller' used to pull the threshing tackle, 1930. © Oxfordshire County Council Photographic Archive.

to keep the sun off my neck, but refused point blank to wear it after the boys called out, "Who stole the donkey, the girl in the white hat!" We only heard about corn dollies and how they were made out of the last sheaf of corn and buried in the field to promote a good harvest the following year; the practice probably went out with the advent of the binder. Before the time of the binder, they had to tie each sheaf with bag-tie before shocking them, which was making a 'wigwam' of eight to ten sheaves so as to prevent the ears of corn from getting wet, as then the rain ran down the stalks.

The aftermath of the harvest was the threshing. We would greet with awe the arrival of the massive steam engine and the threshing machine that was hired out. The whole operation was surrounded in a whirl of dust and flying chaff as the men loaded the grain into big sacks. This was no place for children to play, but we were always sorry when the great steam engine drove majestically out of the farmyard, trailing its pink coloured threshing tackle behind. We had the same affection for what we always called the 'old steam roller', when it was commandeered to level the flint stones in the road which Dick Spicer, our road man, had carefully laid. He was a highly respected member of the community and we children always called him Mr Spicer.

The Farm Labourers

There seemed to be some competition between the carters and the dairymen: both sure that their job was the more important one. My vote was of course for the horses: how could they do the haymaking and harvest without them, let alone ploughing a straight furrow to plant the corn? I somehow didn't consider the cows, whose milk I enjoyed.

Old Tom Newell was the head carter and he was usually pretty miserable. Looking back I can now understand: his wife had died and his young son, Perp, had fallen when he was a baby causing him to be a hunchback with a distorted, overlarge head. So Tom's elder daughter looked after the family and she was pretty miserable too. I used to see her bringing her father a hot meat and dumpling pudding in a basin tied round with a large red Paisley square whenever he was ploughing down the fields. To me he had redeeming features: apart from our mutual care for horses, he always greeted me with the words, "Well done Mildred!" The bother was I never knew what to reply. "Hello" would not have been appropriate, nor "Morning" and certainly not, "Well done Tom!"

Old Tom Dennis was the head cowman and has already been written about in my father's story of him trying to kill the cat that had stolen his milk. He once complained to my father about Monty. He said, "He's a-making faces at me," an accusation which Monty strenuously denied, even to this day. Perhaps it was paranoia, but it was difficult to greet him with a cheery smile, he seemed as miserable as Old Tom Newell. It certainly was a hard life, getting up well before five o'clock every morning, day in day out, whatever the weather. The under-cowman, Gilly Colwell, was just the opposite with his cheery smile and wry humour, but then he hadn't had a lifetime of drudgery. He would always pass the time of day with me and seemed interested in my opinions and I always went to see him milking, even if he squirted a jet of milk with deadly aim to my face. But I have written about that elsewhere.

The most contented of the labourers was undoubtedly Old Guvnor Higgs, the day man, and although he was a master craftsman in the many facets of his work, he was considered by the carters and the cowmen as lower down in the unwritten hierarchy. This did not seem to bother him, he seemed to take a pride in his skill at building hay and corn ricks, thatching, fencing, hedge laying and a host of vital tasks to keep the farm running. He had a passion for fishing, according to Monty, and he managed to get Monty and Perp to collect bumblebees in a jam jar to act as bait for bass. He would get up at four thirty in the morning and walk the mile to the river Cherwell, cutting down a long slender willow 'rod', tying a long string to it with a hook for the bumblebee, which he bobbed to skim the water, attracting the unsuspecting bass. Then he would always clock in punctually for his work as a day man, which fortunately was at seven o'clock rather than the crack of dawn.

There were also a series of farm pupils living in the farmhouse and learning the whole process of farming; later they would hope to rent farms of their own. Philip Nichols stands out in my memory, as he could never wake up in the morning, certainly not at five o'clock to milk the cows. Strident alarm clocks only woke me in the next bedroom and left him sound asleep. They finally hit upon the brainwave of tying his big toe with a string that descended into the courtyard below, where Tom Dennis, guided by his hurricane lantern, would give it such a tug that it would pull him out of bed. This worked once, but the next time the knot round the toe slipped off miraculously, leaving Tom Dennis sprawling on the ground below. Of course it was Phil Nichols who had tied the knot.

Phil was quite a draughtsman and he managed to express in art what he felt about the two Toms, who did not take kindly to this 'layabout'. One instance was a life-like portrait of Tom Newell with a miserable face and the caption, "Who's been missing his Kruschens?" which we all knew as an ad for Kruschen Salts. The sketch was pinned up in the chaffhouse for all to see, until Tom tore it down.

Phil was passionate about breeding ferrets and when there was a new litter he would care for them and the mother in a protective paternal way. I was also fascinated by the newly born creatures: they were red to the point of being almost translucent, blindly squirming around the nest. Gazing above them, I wondered what they would do if they were separated from their mother and was carrying out this experiment when Phil came thundering in from behind. I was so absorbed in their intensified efforts to reach the comfort of the nest that I hadn't heard him come. He was beside himself with anger and I hadn't a leg to stand on. I felt deeply ashamed.

There were other farm pupils: one at a time being looked after by my mother and Aunt Gert. They had enormous appetites and appreciated my mother's cooking. Later they all seemed to marry farmers' daughters from the village or nearby.

The Farm Buildings

The farm buildings were an endless source of discovery for me; I would wander through the stable, past the enormous carthorses to the chaff house, where I could slither and slide down the chaff and run my hands through the great bin of oats.

On to the barn to have a go at turning the handle of the mangold cutter, producing delicate slices for the cow's feed. I dared not enter the small dark room opposite, where a man had been laid after his death – of what? I never knew – death was talked about in whispers. The other half of the barn could be lightened up by two pairs of enormous doors – wide and high enough for the piled-up wagonloads of hay. The rest of the barn was stacked up high with loose hay, which I could roly-poly down. It was there, in one dark corner, that Monty and Perp Newell started pelting something dark with bits of mangolds.

I suspect that they had been afraid to approach it head on. Apparently the dark mass suddenly rose up, cursing them to high heaven. It was one of the many tramps who passed in and out of our lives and who found the hay in the barn a good place to spend the night. We always gave them thick slices of bread and dripping and hot cocoa when they came to the door asking for food, although we knew that they left a chalk mark for their fellows to know that we were a soft touch.

I always gave a wide berth to the engine room alongside the barn; it was stacked with all the machines, which were greasy with oil and only saw the light of day when it was the season for their use. But I had another reason to shun this uninviting place. This was my dark secret, which I have kept to this day. I must have been about seven years old when Jack Higgs offered me tuppence to have a look at me 'down there'. I was sorely tempted and fell. I calculated the tuppence would buy five butterballs, my favourites, a thick stick of liquorice with tiny red balls on top and a pink sugar nougat with a little charm inside. We went into the dark machine shed and he kept his word about only looking, not touching, although I don't think he could have seen much.

When we emerged, I had a problem: where to hide the tuppence? I was sure that my parents would know what I had been up to if they saw it. Jack helpfully suggested that I could hide the two-penny pieces in the opening of one of the hollow pipes stacked against the pigsty wall. They presented a multitude of hiding places in their recesses. He said that when I wanted to go to Mrs. Dennis's sweetshop I could take them out. I thought this was a good idea and also agreed that I should not be seen coming from the buildings with him. So I stuffed the coppers up one of the pipes and went off with a certain pride in my very first earnings. But when I came to claim my booty I couldn't find it, although I thrust my little hand right to the back of every single pipe.

But these guilty connotations with regard to the gloomy engine room were soon forgotten when we played in the three granaries above the barn and the wagon shed. The first was approached from the outside by wide stone steps. Here there were masses of sweet Blenheim apples lasting until Christmas in spite of our continual raids and the fair number that had gone to rot over the months, the grown-ups being far too busy to keep a strict eye on them.

The second interconnecting room was the main challenge to my daring. It was not enough to wade knee-deep in the boxed-off space which held the grain, I had to make myself climb the awesome vertical ladder down to the barn thirty feet below, being quite convinced that it was going to give way from its fastenings and land me on the concrete floor underneath it. I have described this elsewhere together with the biggest challenge to my courage or, more aptly, my stupidity. This was the famous jump from the crane opening down on to the wagon filled with hay.

It was with a sense of relief and accomplishment that I would climb up the plinth to the last long room and here were all sorts of treasures, stored in a great chest with drawers at the bottom and wardrobe above. It was a paradise for us to play at dressing-up in old-fashioned clothes and our favourite make-believe, which was 'houses', with a delicate china tea set and a host of knick-knacks for which there was no room in the farmhouse.

Although I was revolted by the smell, I couldn't help venturing into the men's lavatory. It was the graffiti that attracted me, having learnt to read. Some I understood, like, "Martin, Martin, Fell down farting, Got up stinking, Went away blinking." It was a silly verse that all the village children knew. Then there was one, "Please study economy and use both sides of the paper." I didn't know what the word 'economy' meant, but I had a poor view of such a study. Finally there was a message, "Blocked again! You can't get a four inch turd down a two inch pipe." The plumbing deficiency was beyond me, but one thing was certain: it was indeed blocked again. I suppose I can say that my continual explorations on the farm gave me some insight into the many sides of human life.

The Carthorses

Of all of the animals on the farm, it was the carthorses that impressed me most and I was as frequent a visitor to the stables as to the Blacksmith's shop. I was quite in awe of them as they towered high above me in their stalls. The most intriguing thing about them was the quantity of pee they produced, only equalled to the mountains of shit, in 'bumbles' as we called them, forming pyramids surrounded by a haze of steam. At a young age I wasn't aware of the benefits of manure for roses, but now I understand why our rose trees produced such amazing blooms. But it was the pee that made me step back to keep my distance, as although the carthorses seemed to escape getting splashed by putting their legs well apart, like peasant women in the old days, the sheer force of their output would somehow ricochet off the concrete floor on to wherever I was standing. All of these activities were accompanied by what sounded like thunder and near at that!

Apart from the magnitude of their natural functions, the carthorses were a fairly docile lot, presumably after centuries, if not millennia, of domestication. There were five of them. The most frisky was Blackbird, who was quite a brash, young stallion, and although he was gelded he bore himself with a masculine type of aplomb, as he tossed his flowing mane when he galloped round the Close at the end of the day. But the self-appointed conquering male was Ventnor, a name presumably handed down from the Roman conquest; he asserted his superiority by continually stamping on the concrete, straw-strewn floor.

Flower was always referred to as 'Old Flower'; it seemed as though she had always been mature and was now certainly beginning to feel her age when out ploughing. This is why she was always allocated to me when I tried my hand at haymaking; one thing was certain, she would never run away with me! Then there was Betty. She was young and beautiful and as delicate as a carthorse can be with light chestnut coat and darker mane and tail. She was compliant and took all of her duties in an energetic stride.

But the real aristocrat was Diana, a cob who had belonged to John Buchan no less. She had developed a slight limp and was more suited to my father's gentle routine of going round the fields. She was white, or grey as one is supposed to say, with some really grey dappled markings. Although she had quite stalwart legs, she had an air of delicacy and to me she had a touch of magic. This was when I had climbed up our 'King Charles's oak' and then couldn't get down again; my father must have heard my cries and he came galloping (in my version), it was probably a gentle trot in reality, to rescue me. As I was gently lowered to safety and brought home astride Diana in front of my father, I was a fairy princess and had been rescued by my prince!

Here I must pay tribute to my father's understanding and encouragement of my need to free myself from the stereotype of the woman's role; in fact he treated me as he would a boy: he assigned to me 'Old Dot' who must have come with the farm when we moved to Elsfield when I was three. Dot was

always 'Old Dot' and I have the image of her as being forever forty years old, which are the very last years of a horse's life. No way could a small child be in danger with her, except in sliding off, as she would suddenly put her head down as she spied a choice bit of grass. She was almost as broad as she was high and being on her back would have been good practice for the splits for any aspirant acrobat. My inclination was more of a circus turn and I practised ardently standing on her broad beams as she

The 'King Charles' oak where my father rescued me when I could not get down.

meandered along. She seemed to sense that anything more than a slow walk was inappropriate, whereas I saw myself as doing the graceful balancing act on a cantering steed to the applause of spectators. 'Old Dot' lasted until I was about eight and then she was laid to rest not a moment too soon. Father then bought me Darkie for £15.00, which was a great deal of money in the twenties, and to my shame I kept quiet about the Barclays home safe where I had been saving up for a pony. He never reminded me of it.

Father talked about animals like humans. He knew that if you put a calf into a field where the other calves had been there for some time, they would all chase him round and round the field. When that one had grown older and another calf was put in with them, he was the biggest bully of all.

Billy the Bull

Our immense bull was not in my orbit in the early years; he was always in his pen, well cloistered from the cows, except when they 'wanted to go to the pictures' in the Oxfordshire euphemistic jargon. This the cows indicated

by 'playing piggy back' to another reluctant cow. When I saw the real thing for the first time, I was fascinated and called my mother to watch the bull playing piggy back in the yard. I was quickly hustled in the house without a word of explanation, and so my slow realisation of the sexual mysteries began.

When I was a little older, I would dare myself to creep past the dark passage next to the shed where the bull was incarcerated and he would roll his eyes, rattle his chains, stamp his feet and go backwards as far as his chains would allow. I was terrified, but still retained a 'frisson' of power from being able to look him in the eye from my position of safety.

My father had brought up 'Billie', as he was affectionately called, from calfhood; hence he had a misplaced sense of security in their relationship. One day when he went in as usual to give him his hay and an affectionate slap on the rump with the confident words, "Get over then Billie," he found himself tossed up on to the beam, where he clung shouting for dear life! Finally, Jimmy Colwell, the under-cowman, heard his cries and warded off Billie with a two-pronged fork, with all the verve of a Spanish bullfighter, while father climbed down over the manger to safety. I think that there were no more slaps on the rump after that.

Thus I was brought up to have a wholesome fear of bulls. Other farmers kept them in the fields with the cows, which was presumably more satisfying all round, except to me. Once we children were walking alongside a hedge when we realised there was a monstrous bull in the herd of cows in the field and what is more he was already snorting and pawing the ground with a view to a charge. We ran until we could shoot through the thick hedge, getting horribly scratched by the brambles and emerged into what we thought was safety. To our dismay, after a few yards the hedge became an open gap and there was nothing between the bull and us. We froze in fear, but for the bull it was 'out of sight out of mind', and he had turned his attention to the more enticing charms of his harem. But for us we had never run so fast in all our lives alongside the hedgerow!

Later Billie was able to assert himself more positively when Harry French, the under-cowman, braved him in his pen. I was never told the details, but heard snatches of conversation like, "His trousers were slit from top to bottom" and "He had to be stitched up at the hospital as both of them were hanging out!" and "The nurses all had a good laugh." It didn't seem anything to laugh about to me.

By this time my brother, Monty, had no illusions about Billie's intentions and was absolutely scared stiff when he had to tie Billie up and get him in the cart to take him to Banbury market to be sold, as he was getting a bit too 'raughty'. Somehow they got a rope round him through his nose and got him into the cart. But the law was that you weren't allowed to tie them up through the nose for the journey in the cattle truck: they just had to have a kind of halter round the neck. There was a moment of sheer terror when Billie was divested of the controlling nose gear and all that was between the men and the bull was a simple rope halter, which Billie could have made into mincemeat. They pictured him breaking the rope and making a last bid for freedom by jumping out of the truck. But Billie had the sense to know that such a leap was beyond him and he resigned himself to the inevitable. My father was waiting to receive him in the safety of Banbury. Was the idea some sort of initiation for my brother? For once I was happy to welcome the traditional role of women.

The Cows

I was drawn to the cowshed during milking time, always at three o'clock in the afternoon. The morning milking was at six, which meant getting the cows in from the fields from five o'clock onwards and, for a good part of the year, it was in the dark with hurricane lamps hung at regular intervals in the cowshed to shed a hazy light on the cows' udders; acetylene lamps would have been much brighter, but paraffin for the hurricane lamps was much cheaper. Needless to say, I never experienced this shift. The lighting was always with lamps as there was no electricity in the village for many years, except the

Buchans who had their own plant, which made a constant noise. The cowmen always wore ochre-coloured cotton smocks, far removed from the traditional embroidered smocks that all farm workers wore years ago. When I was at the teachers' training college, we were obliged to make and embroider replicas in linen. I sold mine. Very old people in the village were able to remember the smocks and also the hiring fair at the Wednesday cattle market, when sheep's wool was worn for a shepherd, whipcord for a carter or groom, and a corn dolly for a general farm worker.

The cows all had names, which the cowmen all knew, but my relationship with them was minimal. I liked to watch the men milking from my wary stance near the cowshed door. I had good reason to be cautious, as they were masters at aiming with deadly accuracy a stream of milk right into my face! As quick as lightning, their greasy caps, worn back to front, would revert to their rhythmic pulling of the teats, which gave notes of high pitched music as the squirts of milk echoed against the metal buckets and then, with an air of great innocence, ask me if I liked milk. They knew the personalities of all the cows and rated them both with regard to their kicking propensities and also for their milk yield. The queen in this respect was Strawberry, who was a blue roan Hereford, and her mottled markings of a pinkish mauve were indeed like an overripe strawberry. One incident stands out in my memory: I went skipping down the yard as usual to the cowshed where Jimmy and Gilly Colwell were milking, their heads nestled into the sides of the cows, wearing their caps back to front so that the peaks didn't get in the way. When I came bouncing in, they twisted their heads round to look at me without stopping. It was my sixth birthday and I proudly announced the fact and Gilly Colwell said, "And what will you be like when you're sixty?" looking at me with his impish blue eyes. I was curiously moved, as it was the first time I had contemplated any sense of continuity with older generations and when I actually did reach that unbelievable date, I remembered Gillie and his ready humour. I expanded on my grownupness by confiding in him that I could do up my buttons and he asked what I thought to be a sensible question, "Yes, but can you unbutton them with one hand?" This occasioned some raucous laughter on the part of the milkers, bent over their stools. I couldn't see that it was that funny, but promised Gillie that I wouldn't tell my father about it and, as ever, I was left with a bewildered idea of the inexplicable behaviour of adults.

With Dot, I could more easily realise my great joy in 'helping' on the farm, especially when I could accompany my father riding down the fields. It was empowering to fetch the cows up for the three o'clock milking. I would face any rogue cow that wanted to duck back in the opposite direction. From the safety of being on Darkie, I would brandish a stick and shout, "Cup, cup, cup" (halfway between 'cup' and 'coop'). Any rebel would be inclined to face Dot and me head on with a menacing lowering of the horns and then think better of it and gallop off in the right direction.

The sheep could be more docile, but occasionally a recalcitrant one would dart off in the wrong direction and then the whole flock would rush to follow her. Hence our local expression, "as silly as a ship." It was only later that I realised that they were referring to 'sheep' and not to an impersonal boat. We did not call, 'Cup' or 'coop' for the sheep, they were treated with a resonant, "Ho, ho, ho!"

The sheep provided an extra excitement to me at the yearly sheep dipping. They were all hustled, several at a time, into a long, narrow trough full of chemical dip, which would kill any bugs. The bit I liked was encircling their necks with pitchforks to make sure their heads had been completely immersed. It did not get rid of the worms however and one of my jobs was to squeeze them out of the sheep's skin. I must confess that I found this satisfying, rather like squeezing a spot, but with none of the consequences.

Chapter 3

The Village School

Miss Stace – Headmistress

It is right that the chapter on the school should begin with a tribute to Miss Stace, who was Headmistress during the time I was there and for many years afterwards. She was the heart and soul of our little village school, lifting it outside the narrow confines of school hours to make it the very hub of the community.

She and her family were devotees of the Cecil Sharpe movement, which enjoyed great popularity in the 1920s and '30s in reviving the traditional folk culture. Oxfordshire still stands high in the ranks of preserving the old traditional folk art and this is largely due to the efforts and enthusiasm of people like the Staces.

We children were caught up in her enthusiasm and we always took part in the country dance competitions. We would pile into her bull-nosed Morris and she would take us to Islip or wherever we were competing. Once, when

Photograph above: Elsfield School 1905. From left to right: the 'big room', the infants' room and the men's club. © Oxfordshire County Council Photographic Archive.

the finals were at Woodstock, she treated us to lunch at the Bear before our performance. We were duly impressed with our unaccustomed surroundings and when the supercilious waiter whisked Miss Stace's half-finished plate away, when she had put her knife and fork down for a moment, we were truly in sympathy; we felt she was one of us.

So off we went to the country dance festival. We knew we wouldn't win: it was a foregone conclusion that Bampton always won and so there were no feelings of failure, and I believe that they are top of the league today. We took great pride in our braid colours, which were red and blue and even felt sorry for other villages that hadn't got that combination.

The team would sometimes be invited to tea at her house in Headington; there were three hundred new houses being built on wasteland along the London Road and we would sit happily on the rough grass, which was designated to be their garden, consuming a mountain of home-made cakes and admiring the tricks of her terrier. At her command he would toss a sugar knob from his nose right up into the air and then catch it with a resounding snap!

Her family were always in attendance: her gentle parents, her father who had previously been a headmaster, her brother, presently a headmaster, and her sister Marjorie, also a teacher. I would wonder if Mabel, Miss Stace to us, and Marjorie had ever had a sweetheart or whether their true loves had never returned from the trenches of the First World War, like so many other unmarried women at that time.

It was her enthusiasm that initiated many of the social activities in the village, ranging from the Girls' Friendly Society to the maypole celebrations

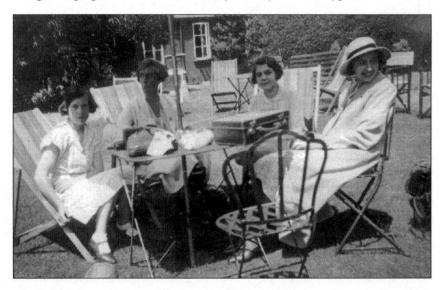

Gladys Hambidge, Miss Stace, Did Warner and Hilda Warner.

and the medieval pageants. Her kindly face and large grey eyes belied the power of her personality and her control of her quite powerful motorbike was an indication of her authority when it came to dealing with obstreperous boys who were even taller than she was. Later she progressed to her bull-nosed Morris with no less command.

Mrs Cox – Infants' Teacher

There was a great contrast between Miss Stace and Mrs. Cox and yet apart from a few times when their differences exploded, they worked in harness together, rather like a couple of carthorses.

Mrs. Cox was a little, rather angular woman with a longish nose and dark fuzzy hair pulled back in a bun, severely controlled with numerous hair pins. It is only in retrospect that I realise what a heavy workload she had. She would cycle from Woodeaton every day with her baby, Eileen, in a basket on the back of her bicycle; it must have been heavy going to push it up Elsfield hill in the mornings, with the possible compensation of whirling down on the way home after school.

She had a son, Reg, and an older daughter, Ethel, so there was plenty of work to do when she arrived home. When he was adolescent, Reg accidentally set himself on fire with an acetylene lamp and the whole village was aghast with the details of how the grafted skin would not join over his chest, making him permanently bent.

Mrs Cox could have had little time to prepare an adequate lunch for herself and she seemed always to be eating tins of fruit even in the classroom. Once she left unguarded a tin of pineapple half empty and two of us soon tucked into the rest. "Has anyone eaten my fruit?" "No Miss." She did not pursue what would be a useless inquiry and was soon heralding us in after playtime with such stirring tunes as 'The brave old Duke of York' with all of her force at the piano, which may have been therapeutic.

She kept a knife handy to peel apples, which she consumed with obvious relish during our play times, and when, as an infant, Did Warner saw it, she chipped all the way along her desk. Miss Stace was sent for from the big room and, in spite of her denial, they found out in the end. When she visited the school years later, the gash in the wood was still there. Again much later on, her small daughter did just the same thing and Did remembered how she had done it when she was little.

Miss Hopcroft

I only knew of Miss Hopcroft through hearsay, as she retired as headmistress just before I went to school. From what I heard, "She was 'a regular Tartar'." It is intriguing how global history adds to our vocabulary, usually in the form of pejorative words depicting the enemy. In the same way I was often called 'a little Turk' when I had been misbehaving. Did Warner only had fleeting memories of Miss Hopcroft when Did first went to school. "What is your name?" "Cassie." "From this day forward you will be called Kathleen." To Sonny Phipps, "You will be called Walter – your proper name on the register." She didn't stick with Walter, but she did with Kathleen. The only other encounter Did had was when she tested the infants' knowledge of colours, "What colour is that?" "Blue for true, Miss." "Very good and this one?" "Pink for stink, Miss" for which contribution Did got a clip round the ear and those were her only two encounters with the 'tyrant'. She was spared the cane, which Miss Hopcroft used liberally even for minor offences. This respite was thanks to Ivy Whitesell, one of the big girls, who, when given the cane, snatched it away, put it across her knee and broke it! So in future, Miss Hopcroft reserved the cane for the boys.

These hefty lads were unwilling captives at school, knowing that their previous generation had often got their release by the age of eleven or twelve. They kept up a continual sort of guerrilla warfare against her. They were already stalwart farm workers, although barely into their teens. Their favourite form of retaliation, in response to the endless caning, was to get behind her and 'accidentally' brush her wig off, which drove her into a paroxysm of fury, as she had desperately wanted her secret to be guarded, which of course it wasn't. She lived with her sister in the school cottage and was probably longing to reach the age of seventy when she would retire to find, I hope, some tranquillity elsewhere. Towards the end, she was becoming more afraid of the big boys, who, by then, towered above her and so she preferred to stand them in the corner rather than give them the stick: an indignity which could only exacerbate their tenuous relationship.

Lessons in the Infant School

For me the infant school was a haze of confusion. There was a coloured Alphabet wall chart from which I copied endlessly, making futile attempts at forming the letter 'a' and when I could give them some kind of similarity to the beautifully rounded models on the wall, I could graduate to 'b' and so on. This seemed to take an eternity and my final reward was to start on the Royal Crown Readers and my continued experience of boredom was in deciphering such sentences as 'Ned led Ted'. As I thought that Ned was probably a donkey, it seemed the wrong way round, but by that time I had learnt not to voice my bewilderment.

The rest of the time seemed to be spent in cutting out coloured paper with rebellious scissors and sticking it down to make a pattern; drawing on the wall

Elsefield School: the infacts' class, 1905. © Oxfordshire County Council Photographic Archive.

blackboards with coloured chalks; doing puzzles from old 'Home Chats', and, the most useless: unravelling material to fill cushions, where my non-co-operative contribution would have been insufficient to make one for a doll. I did fare better with the 'ribs' of Plasticine and made little animals – an obsession which has lasted to this day, but now in clay. I believe that the notion of numbers was contained in the manipulation of literally countless beads and dried peas; I had little idea as to what to do with them; the boys did and stuffed them up their noses, sometimes with drastic results. They tried to stuff them up my nose, but I stood resolute and wouldn't let them.

To go into greater detail of my growing sense of inadequacy, this is how I made out on trying to make a woolly ball. I was given a double circle of cardboard with a large hole in the middle and apparently the process was to wind limitless quantities of wool through the hole. After pursuing this course for some time, I felt that there must be a purpose to this 'no beginning, no end' activity and plucked up courage to join the long queue shuffling towards the rather fearsome Mrs. Cox, perched on her high chair like a sharp-eyed bird of prey. As I neared the front of the queue I saw other children coming back triumphantly with their fluffy balls bouncing in their hands, their eyes sparkling with success. My vigil was brusquely interrupted by the teacher, snatching my skimpy ring with barely a half dozen rounds of wool, "Well, what do you want?" "I wanted to know if it was alright, the ring." She looked down at me through her thick spectacles with ill-disguised disgust, "I thought you'd finished" and gave me a not too friendly push towards my little chair. Long afterwards I gathered how exactly this operation turned out to be a woolly ball. I recall that the chairs were indeed little; more suited for toddlers than for strapping five- and six-year-olds. Our little backsides were wedged in them so tightly that they often stuck to us when we got up to walk.

Then there was story time and I took very seriously the story about the wolf swallowing seven little kids whole. If my father had kept goats or if there had been pictures to show that these were animals, not children, my identification might have been one step removed. Even if the mother goat had slit open the wolf's stomach to release the kids and replaced them with big stones, the trauma that those kids must have suffered must have been horrific.

It did seem that at the infants' school all the previous uncertainties and mysteries of life were intensified and these were stamped with the approval of authority in the form of Mrs. Cox. Yet there was one memorable afternoon which did a lot to put my bewildered experiences in a more positive light. This was when all the infants went down the fields to Little Wood, adjoining Long Wood, to go 'nutting'. Mrs. Cox, who was usually tense and impatient, expanded in the warmth of the golden autumn sunshine. She held down the branches, laden with ripe nuts, for us to shake so vigorously that it was like a hailstorm raining over our heads and then we scrambled for the biggest clusters. She suddenly became a benevolent mother figure to me, in place of an authority who towered over my inadequacy in the classroom.

Lessons in the Big Room

Like all other aspects of village life, there was a fairly set pattern to the school day now we had graduated to the big room. It always started with the assembly, which consisted of hymn singing and the boys barking out with gusto, 'Fight the good fight' and 'All things bright and beautiful'; the girls could hardly make themselves heard. Scripture then followed on as a matter of course; we did the gospels and the Acts of the Apostles so thoroughly that I recall most of them today. We all knew the thirteenth chapter of Corinthians by heart: I liked the lines, "Though I speak with the tongues of men and of angels, and have not charity, I am become as sounding brass, or tinkling cymbal." Nowadays we have replaced the word 'charity' with 'love', which is more in keeping with present-day language.

Then it was time for drill, sergeant-major style: in rows, arms stretching forwards, upwards and sideways, touching toes all in unison. Back again for arithmetic, preceded by 'mental', when the ominous words, "One to ten" meant a scramble for our seats and be ready for the first question; this was in fact a good ploy to settle us down after the strenuous drill. Arithmetic was individual working at our own speed through the books and Miss Stace kept a wary eye on any who might be copying and administered her varying brand of punishment.

The release of playtime sent us once more through the infants' room, this time vacated as we were all in the playground together. We all came marching back to the energetic piano playing of Mrs. Cox and, if it was our favourite reading book, we would sing its title as we marched. I recall singing, 'Children of the New Forest' at the top of my voice when we knew that another instalment was waiting for us. The final half-hour of the morning was either Geography or History, made alive with all of Miss Stace's enthusiasm and our artistic creativity in illustrating her lessons. The big room was over two thirds of the whole school, separated from the infant room by a partition that was removable for village social occasions. Noise from both classrooms was taken for granted and everyone had to go past the infants to get into the big room.

After eighty years, it is amazing how much I recall of these lessons. We learnt masses of poetry by heart and it seemed to come very easily and it has continued to be a joy as I now understand something of the depth of meaning in those poems: Wordsworth's 'To Daffodils', or 'How they brought the good news from Ghent to Aix', for example. Tales from history captivated my imagination and still do: how Stephen and Martha escaped from Oxford Tower by putting the shoes of their horses back to front so that it would confuse their pursuers. Geography concentrated on the lives of other children, especially what they had in common with us, and to me there seemed to be a link with the countryside, nature and animals. But I was taught how we were 'superior', being members of the great empire and that they were lucky to belong to it, even though they were not British.

Then we all went home to midday dinner and I had the longest distance to walk. We sang grace before and after, altogether with the infants. I just had time to enjoy my meat and two veg and pudding when I had to catch up with the group meandering back.

The afternoon was devoted to the arts: painting, country dancing, singing and needlework, with gardening instead for the boys. Painting mostly was from nature: sticky buds, wild flowers, autumn leaves and all sorts of birds. Country dancing was geared to the county competitions and we also practised them in the playground. There was 'Gathering Peascods', 'Jenny pluck pears' and lots more.

The boys did Morris dancing but they never practised in their playtime; they liked to be dressed up for the part: white flannels, ribbons with bells round their ankles and the sticks instead of swords which they banged together with great gusto. We used to laugh at Harold Hemmings, who always turned up his eyes to heaven as he danced as if to get some divine blessing. We were all together for singing and shared the whole range, from the sad stories of 'Barbara Allen' and 'Annie Laurie' to the robust 'Grenadier Guards' and 'Men of Harlech'.

I preferred the lilting rhythms of songs like 'Blow away the morning dew' and 'A lawyer he went out one day' and 'The raggle taggle gypsies O'. I would have liked to do gardening and woodwork rather than needlework, but these were for the boys. The needlework was commandeered by Miss Parsons; from her early days she had always been in charge of the distribution of the fabrics: stout calico for the cookery aprons and thick pink flannel for the men's shirts. I toiled over the gussets and buttonholes of a shirt for Monty for months, leaving traces of blood, sweat and tears on the finally finished article, only to find that he would not be seen dead in it!

Mondays were cookery days for the big girls and I was probably the youngest of them; I was quite frightened of our big girls, but the ones at Marston, where we had to go, seemed even bigger. The cookery teacher had advanced ideas on democracy and I was put in charge of organising the clearing up. I felt that I took my life in my hands and ordered the biggest girl to clean the greasy blackened pans, but to my surprise she complied with good grace. Soon she would be in service and compliance would be the order of the day. Cookery mornings had their moments: when the teacher was outside for a moment, we would throw our pastry up to land on the other side of the old beam, or when making pancakes try to get them to stick on the high ceiling. We showed that we were just as capable of 'playing up', which was the boys' prerogative at Elsfield School. Perhaps it was because we were outside Miss Stace's orbit, as she had a strong hold on our behaviour that somehow we trusted. Trailing home from cookery was a long drawn-out affair: there were our shepherds' pies to consume, although the pastry had not been tenderised by its flights and the mutton was full of gristle. But our appetites were whetted after paddling in the Washbrook and we munched them hungrily whilst drying our feet on our coarse cookery aprons.

Then back to the routine of the rest of the week. Sometimes there was a break in the order of things: one that I hated, like hygiene, and ones that I loved, which were the occasional outside practical lessons. Why I disliked the hygiene lessons was because we had to learn about all the organs (well, almost all of them). They were depicted through highly coloured charts, which seemed to me always full of blood. I immediately turned white as a body protest and was sent to sit outside on the white stone, which was considered the ultimate cure against fainting. Looking back it was probably to get me out of the way in case I disrupted the lesson. I was often accompanied by Betty Webb, who, it was said, needed the colour brought to her cheeks. Neither of us ever learnt much about the function of our body parts and to me it has remained a mystery. I still look away when the blood flows on television.

What a contrast to the other lessons outdoors: roaming the fields to collect specimens of flowers, berries and leaves. One real outdoors lesson stands out in my memory, when the infants' section of the school had to be re-thatched. We all lined up outside to hear the wisdom of the thatcher, a day man in the village, as he demonstrated his skill. I am confident that I could still make a good job of thatching if I were put to it! Although of course we were not permitted to climb the ladder and have a go. Later as a teacher I have always been an advocate of practical experience in learning,

At this stage I must pay a tribute to Miss Stace's versatility. We were taught altogether with an age range of seven to fourteen and she taught every subject, even including surveying with a theodolite, which we made in the class and then took to Burnams, the field nearby, and mapped it out with the exact scale measurements. We thought that was wonderful.

Sometimes visitors interrupted the general flow of the curriculum. Regular ones were Miss Parsons, representing the Manor. Although she had long since moved to Home Farm, she still retained her authority. There was also the vicar, the representative of the church. In the old days they would both come every day, Miss Parsons to give an acknowledgement of her presence and the vicar to have the boys, who had behaved badly the day before, lined up for the cane. Apparently the cane often landed on his thigh instead of an outstretched hand and I like to believe that was his tolerance of the common practice of withdrawing the hand just as the cane was descending. My memory of Miss Parsons in the needlework lesson is of her smiling benevolently over me as I struggled with the gussets on Monty's pink flannel shirt. She was obviously so happy to see the fruits of her gifts coming into fruition.

But the visitor who aroused my deepest feelings of anger and injustice was the government inspector (as they were called), who noticed that I wasn't wearing a thimble as I sewed. I suppose she had a point as I was finding the rough calico for my cookery apron quite hard going. I gather that she must have criticised Miss Stace for this apparently serious omission, as, to my horror, my beloved Miss Stace reproached me! I had never been told that I must wear one. Looking back this was the time of 'payment by results' and Miss Stace must have felt threatened. To this day I have never worn a thimble.

The regular visits of the attendance officer caused no great stir as the farm labourers were keen on their children learning to read and write: they knew it was some kind of investment for their future and indeed this was beginning to be the case with opportunities of other kinds of work. It was always understood that there was time out for potato picking and the inspector probably turned a blind eye to the absence of the hefty thirteen- and fourteen-year-olds, who were already working before and after school.

The 'bug-scratcher' came intermittently to search for nits and bugs. We had to keep our heads down on the desk, but we all managed to peep as she put one finger up for nits and two for bugs for Miss Stace to inform the parents. We all knew who the infected ones would be – the ones we called 'scruffy'. Nowadays even the most cleanly washed seem to be invaded when there is an epidemic in the school.

The dentist came round once a year in a caravan. I leave it to Jimmy Maltby to describe his experiences of the visit. "It was horrible when the old dentist came. He used the old reading room. The old drill he used had to be turned by hand and it seemed more painful like that. I always remember the pink buckets of bloody water that we used to have to empty. Old Roy Pinker and me always seemed to get this clearing up afterwards. It really turned you up. It was a good thing I suppose."

Empire Day

If there was one date that we all remembered, it was 'Twenty fourth of May, Empire Day', which we learnt to chant like a mantra. We always celebrated it by a school pageant, with the oldest pupils dressed in a variety of national costumes, clustering around the tallest girl, who was Britannia. She was clad in flowing white robes, but you couldn't see much of them as they were largely covered by an immense Union Jack, which in its turn was superseded by a large oval shield with the Union Jack design which she held in one hand and a sceptre in the other. A glistening helmet added another foot to her imposing height with her hair flowing down in long tresses.

The backdrop was always yet another Union Jack of grandiose proportions, held in place by two of the big boys. Clustered around the Union Jacks were representatives of Scotland – kilt, Wales – black conical hat, Ireland – shawl and bonnet and England – flag of St. George masking everyday clothes. Sometimes England was portrayed by a formidable crusader, almost hidden behind a crossed shield and with a knitted balaclava type of headdress. These impressive occasions were a reminder of how fortunate we were to belong to

Empire Day. The older children in full regalia.

such a powerful empire and we were especially lucky to be members of the mother country, although the rest were also lucky to be members of our great empire. But I had no illusions about our relative positions: I was more equal than them. Now I realise that this feeling of superiority that we were imbued

Empire Day celebrations. I am in the third row, second from the right. Too young to have a costume!

with, handed down over generations, has contributed to present-day racism.

'Rule Britannia' held us in her sway and we sang it with such fervour. I loved all the words; especially 'Britons never, never, never shall be slaves' and 'God who made thee mighty, make thee mightier yet' and I knew which side I was on. Now I appreciate the stirring music of Elgar but not the sentiments contained in the words. At least we were well versed in knowledge that the Magna Carta and Habeas Corpus gave us rights to freedom that were very special.

The Playground

When I first went to school at the age of five the playground consisted of a little patch of concrete on the road side of the building and we all milled together: infants and giants – at least that's how they appeared to me. The big girls dominated it and they seemed to have their gentle rituals of control. Monty confided in me when I was asking about his experiences at school all that time ago: he said that the big girls took his pants down and all spat on his little Willie! I don't know if this was general. With me, they swung me up in the air and then right down between their legs with the question, "See London?" I couldn't think how one could possibly see London from Elsfield anyhow and least of all from that angle. It was some time afterwards that I realised the true significance of that question. The big girls were so imposing with their long spotlessly white aprons with butterfly epaulettes, black stockings and neatly laced black boots and equally long tresses of hair. Within a matter of months they would be in service with the complete loss of their authority. Meanwhile they enjoyed the liberty of the playground and taught us little ones the folklore and traditional games that they themselves had inherited.

There was just room for the long skipping ropes, turning like mill sails for us to jump over, under and in and out, taking turns in a long snakelike queue. Top spinning was a favourite too; I recall that my halfpenny purple top, chalked with rainbow colours, once won a prize organised by Miss Stace. It was only an empty date box, radiant with Eastern splendour, but to me it was a prize possession. These games all came round as regular as clockwork, yet no-one seemed to organise them. Besides skipping and top spinning, there was hopscotch, chalked out on every bit of concrete. The boys' favourite was hoop spinning: they would send them down Elsfield hill at a great rate and once one almost hit a horse and cart.

For me, the traditional folk games we played together were the most joyous. We felt that we belonged – at least I did – especially when we were all chanting in a circle, 'Sally go round the moon' and 'In and out the dusty bluebells'. These co-operative games were possible when a much larger playground was constructed at the back of the school. We played, 'What's the time Mr. Wolf?' and 'French and English', where the French were lined up along the middle of the playground and the English had to get past them running the length to arrive at the other side. This entailed many scuffles and George Hambidge even lost a front tooth on the hard concrete surface. Jimmy Maltby also remembered that game, as someone tripped him up as he was dashing past and he fell right on the concrete and cracked three teeth and, although they tried to fix them, he had to have them out eventually.

As we got older ball games replaced most of the traditional ones; the only drawback was that the balls would persist in going over to Mrs. Maltby's cottage next door to the school and she wouldn't let them have them back. In the long run, she had to return them to Miss Stace, as they were the school's property.

I always felt secure in the playground and none of us had the left-out feeling with no-one to play with as we all joined in together. There was only one time when I felt exposed. All the girls had crowded into one lavatory and Emily Watts was showing her bare bottom and giving a little speech about it, saying it was like the sun. I was petrified, fearing that I might be called upon to do the same thing, but fortunately I was saved by the gong, by the sudden intervention of Miss Stace. She was really angry and ushered us all out like a lot of ninepins. To my relief it was made quite clear to us that a repeat of that behaviour would have unimaginable consequences.

School Discipline

By the time I was promoted to the big school there was less of the philosophy of 'Spare the rod and spoil the child' as in Miss Hopcroft's days. Miss Stace used the cane much more judiciously, having at her command a variety of sanctions. At first she did try to re-introduce caning for the girls and soon met with the same fate as her predecessor. Everyone in the village knew of Ivy Whitesell's courageous action and that is probably what inspired her cousin, Dolly Lafford, to do precisely the same thing. Perhaps that fierce spirit of independence ran in the Lafford family. I am eternally grateful to both the protagonists as I would have been terrified of having the cane, never having been struck or smacked in my whole life.

In terms of discipline, the boys were treated differently from the girls, not only in the use of the cane, but also in the alternatives such as a 'clip round the ear'ole' or twisting the ear: this was speedier and interfered less with the lesson. Miss Stace would wander behind them, scrutinising their futile attempts at such sums as long division of money. In Jim Maltby's words,

"What I didn't like about Miss Stace was that she would walk along the back – we were all sitting in rows two or three to a desk – and she would smack you on the ear, smack! Right on your ear. I've often thought how many people would have gone deaf through her smacking them on the ear. She didn't do it so much to the girls, probably because they didn't get up to such tricks as we boys did. The boys were always getting up to tricks, it's true. We used to play her up a bit: that was the rule in those days." The outstanding terror was little Willie Wingfield: he used to kick Miss Stace on her legs and then make for the door, straight across the road and away home right down the fields. "We used to go after him. Oh, he was a wild one." Willie had a distorted hip and limped badly, but it didn't stop him from running away from school. Apparently for him it was like the frying pan into the fire, as his father used to beat him mercilessly and that's why he finally could stand it no longer and ran away to join the army. Long after that we heard that he had become a postman in Bournemouth; being a postman needs some maths and a good memory, so it shows that Billie had the capacity to master these skills.

The on-going feud between the village boys and the school was fuelled by what educationists call the self-fulfilling prophecy. In other words you become what is expected of you and this was certainly true of some of the sons and daughters of the farm labouring class. In retrospect many of them affirmed this influence. "I remember doing the washing up, that's all." "I wasn't very bright at school." "I don't think you can learn a lot in a village school. The brighter ones got all the attention and if you were a little bit under, you didn't get the encouragement. They used to encourage them to get on if they had a bit of brain, whereas we used to get pushed into doing Miss Stace's garden." "I was probably a bit dense. I was probably dyslexic. Miss Stace never taught me as I was always doing the washing up. Can't spell for toffee." This last contribution was from Bessie Phipps, whose whole family has been labelled as dyslexic, but this was never acknowledged in those days. She was convinced that she was dim and, as she was regularly sent out to do the housework in the school cottage and therefore released from her studies, this apparently confirmed her own diagnosis, as she could never catch up. I am sure that all of her six children would verify that she was not only a loving mother, but a highly intelligent one too.

The boys all complained that they never received the fruits of their work: the vegetables they grew, whether in the formal gardening lessons or extra curricular, which might be lifting the potatoes for lunch or planting peas and beans. Only the boys did gardening and they treated it as a bit of a lark. Miss Stace had to supervise the girls' needlework at the same time as the gardening, going through the infants' room to her cottage. It was not surprising that she found mayhem when she arrived. I recall one time when Monty and Perp Newell stormed into our sedate classroom to a remote corner and proceeded literally to fight tooth and nail for it! They were hotly pursued by a furious Miss Stace, who managed to separate them with all skill of a boxing referee. They had been 'playing merry-come-up' in the garden and had been sent to stand in two separate corners.

Miss Stace's discipline towards the girls was different. Since the breaking of the cane incidents by Ivy Whitesell and later Dolly Lafford, Miss Stace's discipline towards the girls was tempered. The corner and ear twisting were reserved for the boys, but a rough push or a shake from behind were quite effective when she discovered, for example, that Bessie Phipps had copied all the sums from Agnes Warner, but of course could not explain their working when confronted. One instance of equality between the sexes was a measure taken in the singing lesson. She would prowl round with a ruler in her hand to thrust it into the mouth of any unfortunate who wasn't singing with a good open mouth. As a last resort, when she found that the older boys were too tough for her to handle, she could send to her brother's school in Headington where he was headmaster – an initiative that would not get through the red tape today.

She was adept at preventive sanctions, such as confiscation, and once some unlawful possession had been taken away, it was never returned. Most of the boys were streetwise and would never have their catapults on them in the wake of a window being broken somewhere in the village. Monty was the only one who was caught with incriminating evidence although he was completely innocent of breaking windows. Like most of the boys, he used his catapult for aiming at birds and I am glad to say he never killed one. He still remembers a prized catapult that father had got him, "A lovely prong – a beautiful shape, a square Y not just a Y shape, which gave more width. It was dogwood that father had found in the wood and I was ever so proud of it. She never gave it back."

To me Miss Stace's regime was relatively benign; she went to such trouble in making her lessons interesting that there were many less occasions for the sort of disruptive behaviour that demanded a rod of iron. But then I was not an older boy kept against my will, nor was I expected to do the chores in lesson time, nor was I dyslexic.

We were hardly aware of Miss Stace's family responsibilities towards her elderly father and mother, until one day she had to leave us on our own. Before she went she said that anyone who spoke should write their name on the blackboard. There was quite a little Gestapo watching the lips of everyone and demanding that they should write their name, so that what with one accusation and another the board was completely full by the time she came back and we all waited in apprehension. To our surprise, she hardly glanced at the revelations on the board but gave us some work to get on with before she dashed out again. This sobered us more than any reproaches and we sensed the seriousness of the situation. In fact her father died soon afterwards. We had not realised that she was also nursing her father and mother in the school cottage as well as all the rest of her activities.

Looking back on my happy days at the village school, I realise how deep the separation was when I left to go to the Milham Ford School at Oxford. Miss Stace tried to keep secret the fact that she had bought Emily Watts and me a wooden pencil box as a goodbye present, but of course the other children found out. I was confronted with the open accusation of being 'stuck up' and our relationship was never the same again.

Until then we had all played together, except of course the children of the Manor and vicarage, and already the dreaded scholarship exam, the forerunner of the eleven plus, with its divisive powers set out to separate us. In fact all of my generation failed the decisive second part and I feel that Did Warner had a point when she commented that the reason we never succeeded was because the Oxfordshire County Council would have had to provide us with bikes. Her theory only comforted us for a year, after that Gladys Hambidge won the coveted prize.

Fortunately for me, my parents could just about afford the fees of £1 13 6d per term, plus of course the bike. However I was allowed to enter the Oxford City 12 plus and succeed, but my step up this ladder was greatly marred for me by the fact that I was alienated from my former playmates. A gap of almost seventy years went by before I contacted them to help me with this book and so an old wound was finally healed.

Chapter 4

The Village

Elsfield is just a single road on the top of a hill, which overlooks the spires of Oxford. In the village, they always referred to it as the city of sprees and spires; this caught my imagination and my ambition was to find out about the sprees and perhaps to join in them. Whenever I could, I would go the field adjoining Watts's farm and look down on that magical city with spires like castles in the air, except that they were down below. There is a farm at each end of the village and another opposite the church, a few hundred yards from the top of the hill. The school, no longer there, was next to the farm on the hill and the Manor House somewhat in the middle. That's all except for the workers' cottages distributed the whole length of the road, which measures about a quarter of a mile in all.

The village was divided in the middle by 'under elms': great sweeping trees on both sides of the road, their tops almost meeting to form a cathedral-like archway. When we walked past, we would quicken our paces to emerge from the gloom to daylight. This did not prevent us however from playing 'houses' under the elder bushes, which grew prolifically below the canopy, with endless concocting of cakes and puddings made of mud and elder berries. Now with disease striking all elm trees, it is bathed in daylight with little elm bushes trying to reach their former grandeur.

It has none of the attributes of more sophisticated villages – a green or at least a pond or a network of side roads – but in the twenties and thirties, when I was growing up, it was a vibrant community, full of life and activity. Now it is a ghost of its former vibrating spirit. The previous farm labourers' cottages have all been bought up at high prices and their former tenants are mostly in old peoples' homes in neighbouring Marston. The school, which was always the focal point of the village, has long since been closed and then pulled down to reveal an aching gap and the shop and post office also met their fate at the beginning of the Second World War.

This is in no way a plea for wallowing in nostalgia. What would we do today without cars, telephones, washing machines, dishwashers, radio and television – let alone CDs and the Internet? This was the reality when I was

Tom and Perp Newell's cottage.

growing up in the twenties and thirties. There was also a rigid class hierarchy that wouldn't be tolerated today; then we just took our place in the system for granted. There was certainly hardship and hard work, but there was also a spirit of community that was really caring. Today there are growing efforts to rekindle that spirit, as it is all too easy to feel alienated in modern life. The other aspect of life that has been eroded, at least for country people, has been the freedom to roam in the countryside at will, as long as we were not encroaching on the lord of the Manor's domain.

Although money was really scarce, no-one went short of food. All the villagers had quite a bit of garden, the front part radiating a proliferation of country flowers: Canterbury bells, marigolds, lupins, delphiniums and roses in profusion, especially ramblers bedecking the cottage walls. But the real value was in the vegetable plot, supplemented by the allotment, which provided the basis of midday 'dinner' year in and year out. The allotments were doled out to the labourers by the farmers; ensuring that everyone had a fair share. So growing vegetables was the main occupation for the whole family after work and the soil was rewardingly fertile.

I recall my first attempt at digging up new potatoes, I speared quite a few but they still tasted delicious with plenty of butter. The vegetable gardens were almost as colourful as the flower ones, with rows of runner beans up to nine feet high with clusters of bright orange flowers dangling down. There were deep-red beetroots with everlasting foliage, which we could eat all the year round. My overwhelming memories are of the perfumes of the honeysuckle, the old-fashioned roses, the tobacco plants and most of all the whole fields of broad beans cultivated for fodder for the animals.

But it wouldn't be dinner without meat and there were always rabbits, bought from the farmers for sixpence or more likely by poaching, as the labourers were not allowed to shoot them.

The main supply of meat was guaranteed by the nurturing of the family pig. It was fattened up on all kinds of scraps and killed, with not an ounce left uneaten or preserved in salt. I was most distressed to be within earshot of the killing and indeed this was hard to avoid. The piercing squeals could be heard the whole length of the village and I always thought that they were being burnt alive, what with the burning straw and the heart rending shrieks to high heaven. In reality the squealing was when they were being forced out of their sties to the place of execution, where their throats would be cut. They always seemed to have an uncanny foreboding of their fate. The blazing straw was in fact to burn off all their bristles so that the cracking on the joints could be savoured. I used to like the 'chittlins' and fortunately did not know what they were made of.

Everyone had a few chickens that roamed freely during the day and somehow went of their own accord into their pens to roost at night. This was for a daily supply of eggs – chickens were far too valuable to eat and probably rather tough, owing to the amount of exercise they took – although we didn't get the chance to try except at Christmas or Easter.

The cottages were all two up and two down, although the more recent ones had little kitchens and larger rooms and windows. The older ones all had thatched roofs where swallows always nested under the eaves. They were certainly picturesque looking, but often damp and dark. Today they are being bought up and renovated for a more opulent generation. The kitchen-living room had the range which was on all day every day, whereas the parlour was seldom used, containing treasures such as stuffed birds and glittering vases won at the fair.

The Weather

We were very much at the mercy of the weather, which seemed more extreme in those days and I believe it was. In winter we could be cut off from Oxford for days on end when the snow and ice prevented the carriers' carts and pony traps from scaling Elsfield hill. We had to rely on loyal tradesmen who would walk across the snow-covered fields, laden with baskets of bread and essentials.

Floods affected us in the same way. Once, when the Washbrook flooded its banks, we were stranded on our way back from Oxford. It had become a mighty torrent in a matter of hours after a thunderstorm and we were only saved by the coal cart, which could ride the waves like an ocean liner. We had to cling on tight to the bags of coal as there were no protective rails and when we climbed down triumphantly at the top of the hill, we were black with coal dust! It had been a great adventure.

Elsfield, at the top of the hill, was the target for gales, especially from the east; they used to say that there was nothing between Elsfield and the Ural mountains, with the implication that these gales were deliberately aimed at us from Russia. I would boast that the worst gale almost 'got' me as I was battling my way home from school. Luckily Mr. Morbey, Miss Parson's gardener, seemed to appear from nowhere and saw what was going to happen and held my arm with the one word, "Wait!" as he gazed up at an elm tree towering above us, swaying deliriously before it came crashing down just where I would have been! It was an awesome moment and after thanking him profusely, I dashed home saying that Mr. Morbey had saved my life! I experienced a thrill of pleasure to see my parents visibly shocked: it was reassuring to have confirmation of their immense care. My father, who had been sheltering indoors, as little farm work could be done, went off immediately to thank Mr. Morbey and soon the whole village knew of my escape from death!

On another occasion a gale raged with even greater force and the tall trees 'under elms' came down like ninepins and one of them crashed onto Mr. Clark as he was cycling home from work. He died straight away, although they had managed to drag him from under the massive branches. It was Mrs. Hambidge's first day of her new village shop and she said that having a dead body brought in was the last thing she expected. Later we learnt that Mrs. Clark, his widow, would have no compensation as it was 'an act of God'. I found it difficult to understand why God had committed that particular act and couldn't help feeling relieved that he hadn't had to do the same for me. I associated God very much with the Grand Arbiter of the weather; we always would pray for fine weather for haymaking and harvest and some people even prayed for sunshine for their picnics. That's alright, I thought, as long as someone else doesn't gum up the works by praying for rain at the same time. I felt that it must be very difficult for Him to know what to do.

There were also long hot summers and there were several cases of sunstroke. The gardener at the Manor died after taking the water in the horse-drawn water cart down to the allotments backwards and forwards all day long. There had been such a drought that water was actually rationed – a rare phenomenon in those days.

Carrier's cart in the Banbury district, 1910. © Oxfordshire County Council Photographic Archive.

Carrier's Cart to Oxford

There was only one system of public transport to Oxford and that was by carrier's cart on Wednesday, Friday and Saturday. There were three carriers: the Lambournes, the Brewertons and Old Mr. Willis. They were all privately owned and presumably financially viable, at least until there was a bus service and then they disappeared overnight and not even to reappear when years later the bus service was cancelled. They were gone forever.

The cart was not unlike a smaller version of the Western covered wagon with bench seats all round inside and a permanent canopy covering it. We children were sent to look out for the carriers and before they were in sight we could hear the rumbling of the metal wheels on the flint stone road. It was quite difficult to get up the precarious wooden steps to the cart and when we were installed it was really wobbly, especially when the stones in the road made the cart lurch. It cost 2d to go to Oxford and back, with children free and each of the three carts could hold ten people.

It took about an hour to get to Circus Yard at Oxford and then we would have to get back there by three o'clock to be in time for tea at home. Coming back took a bit longer than going, as the ascent of Elsfield hill caused us to climb out and, in the case of some energetic folk, help the horse by giving a shove to the solid cart. Could this have helped? Such a calculation was and still is completely beyond me, but it established an empathy with the weary horse

Carrier's cart, Banbury Museum.

cob straining away at the heavy load, which was at least relieved of the weight of the passengers.

The carriers would do much of the shopping for the villagers. The Brewertons were a particularly warm-hearted couple, who would go to a lot of trouble to buy a special purchase: a wick for the cowshed lamps or a yard of muslin to strain the redcurrant jelly. They were even known to go to meet visitors arriving by train at Oxford station, identifying them according to the description given. Jack Brewerton was said to have an eye for the ladies; he certainly helped them down with utmost courtesy and teased us girls as we jumped down sometimes into his arms. He was a cheerful soul and certainly made the journey a jovial affair.

Not so Mr. Willis; he always seemed grumpy and made the passengers feel uncomfortable. We children called him 'old grizzle pot'. His method of delivery was to open the door, which was never locked, call out 'carrier' and then throw the parcels onto the floor! I never knew how it was decided as to which one we travelled with; they all came from the village of Beckley and maybe most of the places were taken by the time they meandered through Elsfield. We always considered ourselves unlucky if we landed up with Mr. Willis and, as a child, I could sense immediately that he had little time for youngsters. This view was amply reinforced when I had the misfortune to rest my weary feet on a pound of 'best' butter – at least that is what I was informed as to its quality. In my opinion there wasn't much harm done: a wriggling of the greaseproof wrapping paper which bore minute traces of Oxford mud and a tiny tear where a little speck of butter was oozing out. But my opinion was not called for, nor did I have the opportunity to ask what it was doing on the floor anyhow. I would be more sympathetic today; he would have to face the customer waiting for her best butter and he apparently had no wife to give him comfort, as did the Lambournes and the Brewertons. All I sensed that he was even more grumpy for the whole journey from Oxford and I was made aware that I was the cause of it.

One memory strands out in my mind was of an old woman dressed in black who was a frequent passenger from Beckley; she always wore a black pointed hat, as if determined to the be mistaken for a witch. Her nose and chin seemed to be on the same curve almost meeting each other and her hands were thin and claw-like. I couldn't take my eyes off her, even when I heard my mother say to a neighbour, "Look at our Mil, staring at that old woman." Did I really think that she was a witch? It certainly entered my head and I confess to a shiver of apprehension, so I always saw to it that my mother was firmly wedged between her and me.

Ponies and Horses

Our dependence on the horse far exceeded the weary old cobs that drew the carriers' carts. Our main form of transport was at least an equestrian tribute: 'Shanks's pony'. Who was Shanks, I wondered and why did I never see his pony, which carried so many people about? The farmers all went on horseback to supervise the workers: Mr. Watts on his powerful charger, Mr Hatt on a light bay and my father on Diana, the white cob. The rest of the villagers walked everywhere, especially to Oxford and back. They said, "The miles and miles we walked!"

Pony trap, mostly used for social occasions. It was always my favourite.

I was endlessly fascinated by all sorts of variation of pony carts. The most elaborate was the one actually driven by the two Holland-Hibbert young girls, who came from the Manor at Beckley every day to share the Buchan's governess. Our milk float was at the lowest ebb of the market; it was basically to carry churns and you had to vie with them to squeeze yourself a place. As my adored Gillie Cowell was driving the milk float to Oxford, I would gladly forgo any discomfort. But this pleasure was abruptly curtailed when he got caught by the police for driving under-age. He seemed very grown-up to me, but he must have been under sixteen and this incident caused my father some trouble.

I have one cherished but dim memory of being in a lovely pony trap with velvet seating and a warm waterproof cover with a scratchy fur underside in the design of leopard spots, which tickled my legs. It was fitted round our laps and hooked to the sides of the trap, so that from the lap downwards we were as dry as a bone, but we needed umbrellas when it rained. We kept that leopard cover for years until it was thoroughly mangy, but the actual ride to Oxford is bathed in mystery for me.

Horses were as well attuned to the rhythm of their work, as were their drivers or riders. Jimmy Maltby's horse always knew which shops he should stop at: whether Liptons or the Home and Colonial. He was only caught out once when he did his usual quick turn into St Clements and suddenly found himself and the cart inches away from a very large bus; they were starting to build a new by-pass which neither Jimmy nor his horse had catered for. Another time some of the 'townies', as we called them, cottoned on to the special click that Jimmy made when he wanted his pony to go on. When Jimmy came out of Woolworths in Cornmarket his pony and cart were nowhere to be seen; they had finally landed up in the middle of Carfax, the central crossroads of Oxford, not knowing where to turn, after his horse had responded to the familiar click. The same thing happened in St. Aldates, when he found a bemused pony in the hands of a policeman.

Although I loved having rides in any kind of cart, wagon or pony trap, it was the joy of having a pony that was central to my life. I would canter and gallop across the fields and trot along the roads with a wonderful feeling of complete freedom, even when I landed head-first on the ground, which was not infrequent. I first inherited the elderly, tub-like Dot and when she finally expired my father bought me Darkie for fifteen pounds. I had been saving up for a new pony in my shiny, oval-shaped home bank, but to my shame, when the surprise pony arrived, I never mentioned my savings and to his great credit my father never mentioned it either, although money was quite tight.

I was never a very proficient rider and as both ponies had inherited a habit

A bike like mine, with a dress guard to stop clothes being caught in the wheel.

of stopping dead in the middle of a fast trop or even a gallop, it took me a number of somersaults to look out for it. With Dot it was always at the sweet-shop, so I ought to have been forewarned; with Darkie it was going up the Beckley road, to which he had an undying aversion and I finally had to come to terms with the fact that this was a no-go area for us.

But the supremacy of the horse was already beginning to wane. Motorbikes were beginning to appear on our previously deserted roads and my father acquired a little two-stroke James, which he rode with great dignity at the daring speed of twelve miles per hour. When it was past its prime, Monty learnt to ride it in the little field, and Mr Higgs was constantly picking up the pieces of the bike that had been scattered. Later the roles were reversed when Monty was old enough to ride a second-hand motorbike. Father had to push-start it and when it finally sprang to life, it ran away with him; so he let go and it careered down the road!

Many of the villagers were by this time buying second-hand bicycles, but for themselves and not for their children. When I was the proud owner of a Raleigh, with blocks fastened on to the pedals, as it was too big for me, it proved to be a double-edged blessing. As I had a bike and the others didn't, I tried to deal with the situation by handing it over to whoever wanted to ride it as I joined the group walking to school. But the difference in our incomes produced a rift that was finally sealed when I started cycling to Oxford to the secondary school.

Playing with Water

My favourite play with the village children was with water: fishing, making dams, bridges and boats and of course just paddling. The Oxfordshire basin was flowing with water: the Thames, the Cherwell and the Windrush all had their network of tributaries, streams and rills. Our favourite was the Washbrook and we would go down the hill to paddle and catch minnows in its crystal water. I was not supposed to paddle, as I was chesty and always seemed to catch a cold afterwards.

I was always found out however, not being possessed of great cunning in my subterfuge. On one occasion we stayed out much longer than usual and my parents must have been worried. When I heard the dreaded pop pop pop of a motorbike. I knew it must be my father, as his was the only one in the village and the steady rhythm of his habitual twelve miles an hour was unmistakable. He always said that it was the pace that killed and we said the accidents were caused by everyone trying to get past him. I had darted under the bridge, standing up to my knees in the Washbrook flow and I heard his echoing voice ask the children, "Have you seen our Mil?" "No" they all lied in unison. Then there seemed an interminable silence – surely it was safe to come out after such a long time. I peered out and in a hushed voice asked, "Has he gone?" "No, he hasn't," and over the edge of the bridge his face mirrored mine. I was then ignominiously carried away on his pillion, clutching my shoes and socks with my legs drying in the wind. This incident like many others tended to alienate me from the farm labourers' children with whom I loved to play, as they were all hale and hearty.

On another occasion, also in the forbidden Washbrook, I was so full of the joie de vivre that I swung on a branch overlooking the stream; it snapped in two and I landed on my back with all my clothes on. Luckily my guardian angel, Bessie Phipps, took me, waddling in my soaking clothes, up the hill to the teacher's cottage where she worked in her spare time and put me to bed naked while she dried my clothes by the stove. My mother was so impressed with her prompt action that she forgot to scold me; by now she had begun to realise that I was drawn irresistibly to water and that even in the small brooks that lined our fields, I would somehow topple over the stepping stones and at least get a shoe full of water. Considering how much extra work was involved when I was bronchial, I realise now how long-suffering she was.

For longer expeditions, I was sometimes tolerated by my brother and his constant companion, Perp Newell, on their trips to Sescut and the river Cherwell. One of the main attractions was to open the gates for motorists where a piece of common land had been fenced off so that the pasture could be grazed. This was their monopoly and they generally got a few coppers from car drivers, motorcyclists and even cyclists, but these travellers to Woodeaton were few and far between, so there were long waits in between each one. I was allotted the pedestrians and I only recall one and he was a tramp, like so many who took to the road in the twenties; not surprisingly I didn't get my tip! I much preferred to be on the banks of the nearby Cherwell, where I could catch minnows and even a gudgeon, which I kept for years in our tank near the cooling house.

Cover-up on Sex

Is there a village collective unconscious? There certainly was an unwritten code as to what could be common knowledge and this implies that there were also unspoken areas. One of these was sex. In spite of being a farmer's daughter in close proximity to our bull, I was brought up in complete ignorance of any aspect of sex. All I knew somehow was that whatever I did in bed was plain wicked and one day (the Last?) I would be found out. Later on menstruation was an unwelcome shock and in adolescence when I kissed, or rather brushed mouths with a farmer's son from Marston, I just wondered if that would give me a baby!

Looking back, I realise that there were hushed whispers, which bewildered me at the time. There was the young farm hand, who asked the girl he was courting if she would have 'pleasure'; when she refused he said that he wouldn't have had her if she'd said yes. That was completely beyond my comprehension; now it seems like sour grapes on his part. I only began to fathom the mystery when I whispered to my friend during the painting lesson at the secondary school, "Why do they do it, if they might have a baby?" She replied, "They like it!" The young man in question could in fact pick and choose. After the First World War there were so many surplus women that it was not easy to get a husband. If a girl went out with a boy who was looked on as inferior to her and eventually married him, there was a common saying at the time, "Arn a one is better than narn a one" and the plight of single women made this only too true.

Another sotto voce account was of a large woman with a grown-up family, who had a baby late in life and there was the question, "Was it really hers?" From my point of view I had never been brought up with the stork myth so I felt that of course it was and couldn't see why there was any doubt. Whispers about her young daughter went right over my head. I seem to have missed out on the only real scandal in the village, when, according Monty, there was a girl who looked like a little cherub who used to work for Miss Parsons and after she was peremptorily sacked, he learnt that all the boys in the village had been 'practising' on her. He expressed regret that it was, "before he could manage it."

The only incident concerning slight abuse of children that I was aware of was when Did Warner was walking under elms at the tender age of eight when a young man got off his bike and kissed her. She ran home crying to her mother who happened to be cutting up meat at the time; she rushed out brandishing her carving knife to get him, but he had long since gone.

Medical Matters

Were we a healthy lot? The fresh air and plenty of exercise together with fresh organic food was a great plus, but the cottages and farmhouses were all damp and the landlords were reluctant to do anything about it. Our house was so damp and draughty that my father had the temerity to tell the landlord, representing Christ Church, that it was not a house but a winnowing machine (one that blows grain in the air to separate the husks from the seeds). It didn't make any difference; no repairs were ever done.

We certainly didn't call the doctor unless it was absolutely necessary, partly because we had to pay and also the practices were some way off, either at Islip or Headington, both entailing a long walk across the fields: once to call him (and doctors were all male) and then again to fetch the medicine. There were strong opinions about the individual doctors. In Jimmy Maltby's summing up, "Dr. Taylor wasn't exactly miserable, but he could never see the funny side and if he thought you were shamming, he told you to get back home and do some work. If you were ten minutes early to call for the medicine, he wouldn't give it out until the exact time. Dr. Arnan, he was a devil! But Dr. Hitchens was the best; he would come out at four o'clock in the morning!"

In the case of emergencies anyone who had a motorbike could be relied upon to help, including Miss Stace if it was one of the children at school. There was quite a bit of pneumonia: Jimmy Maltby got it when he was sixteen and had it three times after that, "It was getting wet-through at work." The whole village followed the progress of those who were ill. I recall the general relief when it was heard that Mr. Morbey had 'passed the corner' with his pneumonia and had managed to eat a boiled egg cooked for just four minutes! On one occasion there was an outbreak of scarlet fever and the children who had caught it were sent to the isolation hospital at Headington and the parents had to walk across the fields just to see their children through a window. I remember a story about my uncle when he went to the doctor who made up his prescription on the spot. The doctor measured the dose with a teaspoon and then went to the tap and filled the bottle with water. "Five shillings please." "Five shillings for that," protested my uncle, "It's almost all water." The doctor said nothing but went to the sink and poured it down, saying, "Help yourself!"

Superstition

There was surprisingly little superstition in the village. There were just one or two ghost stories, rather discounted by the revelation that they were only emanating from Hubert Webb, who tried to frighten people by putting a sheet over his head and wandering under elms giving out weird cries! But Mrs. Charlock, the cook at the Manor, reckoned that she had seen a ghost in the kitchens and in the passages. Some said that she was influenced by the mysteries in John Buchan's books, which sometimes were related to the community, as in 'Fremantle', when the heir to the throne was hiding in Stow Wood near Islip hill. Did we really believe that Queen Elizabeth said, "I slip" on a frosty day at Islip? It didn't seem very likely to me, especially as it didn't sound very good English. And then there was the oak tree just down the road from our farm, where King Charles was supposed to have hidden. I had thought it was Charles the First, instead of the Second, and that he was trying to escape being beheaded. But then every village seemed to have a King Charles Oak. More likely was the belief that the thatched cottage on the way to Forest Hill was once a sort of Wayfarers' house, which harboured high-waymen, who would hold up the coach on the lonely strip before you get to Forest Hill.

The one superstition that I had sympathy with was the effect of Rhode Island Red cockerels chasing and even attacking people. They certainly attacked me, flying right into my face, which wasn't far to go. I was too frightened to face them and they were definitely stronger than me; also I soon learnt that running away was just what they regarded as a challenge to see who could run the faster, so I had to give their part of the farmyard a wide berth. The superstition was that if they attacked a pregnant woman, the image of a Rhode Island Red cockerel would appear on her newborn baby – at least I escaped that! But when Florrie Maltby was expecting, she was chased by this breed of cockerels as she was going up the fields to take her husband's dinner in a pudding basin to the hay field. But I never heard the outcome. I wondered if the chickens' diet of potato peelings laced with red powder to make the hens lay, made the cocks more aggressive.

The only other superstition seemed to be connected with the dead who were always kept in the parlours of the cottages before the coffins were carried away to the church. There was an eerie feeling whilst the bodies were in the house and when Bessie Phipps was left to wash up the cups when Miss Stace's mother was lying dead in the next room, she was convinced that there was some spirit moving the cups as they gently glided down the sloping wash board, which was probably steeped in water. The only superstition that dates from my childhood that I still adhere to is never to leave knives crossed, as that meant fighting in the family. There is one village that I did not consciously recall, but it must have played an important role in my life. Throughout my childhood I heard references, mostly veiled, to something that 'was going on' in a village about four miles away. There was talk in the family of men and women bathing 'with nothing on' in the lake and references to an artist who was, 'no good, a drunk', and about a cousin who married him and had a baby. There was the certainty that no good would come out of it. It was only years later that I learnt that the village where I spent the first two years of my life at a very small farm, was none other than Garsington, the centre of the Bloomsbury set with Lady Ottoline Morrell reigning supreme over it. Recently I saw the aforesaid artist's paintings at the Barbican. The village predictions were fulfilled: he did leave her and later she became paralysed by an attack of polio.

The village must have been imprinted on my sub-conscious as, once when I saw a photograph of a beautiful Manor House, I knew I had been there before and it turned out to be Garsington Manor. My grandparents had lived there for generations and there were various cousins, all farmers, yet I had not ventured that far afield since the age of two!

Chapter 5

The Manor, the Church and the Shop

The Manor

The village still bore traces of the feudal system in the first quarter of the twentieth century. I would hear of how the banker, as Mr Parsons was called, used to go to Oxford to the Old Bank every morning in his dog cart. This was brought to the front door at 9 a.m. by his coachman and groom, with the butler at the door to see him off. For leisure they would ride out in their carriage and pair with the coachman and groom in attendance and also the footman behind. If they ever passed the village children, the girls had to curtsey and the boys bow. The old lord of the Manor, Mr. Thompson of Thompson's bank in Oxford, was a 'regular tartar' according to the older village folk who remembered him. They all went in fear and dread of him as their livelihood depended on his judgment. He had very strict ideas about the curse of alcohol and made sure that the men behaved according to his edict: namely that drink for the working class was evil, he himself being teetotal. He would keep more than a watchful eye on the farm workers as they trooped down to Marston to the nearest pub a mile away, to treat themselves to a pint of beer or more at a penny a pint. Those unfortunate enough to live past the Manor House which bordered the road, had to run the gauntlet on their return. Mr. Thompson had placed a huge mirror in his room facing the street to be able to spy on the returning drinkers. They could only see the back of his head above his armchair and thought that if they stopped singing and took their boots off, he wouldn't hear them. So with great hushing and loud whispering advice about making no noise, they were caught all too often in the mirror which he was watching like a hawk.

The next morning those who had been spotted were summoned to receive a severe warning and warned of their sins and, if it happened a few times, they

The old Manor House where Miss Parsons lived. The daffodils carpet the lawn.

were dismissed and then they were not only jobless but also homeless as well, as they had to vacate their tied cottage to make way for their replacement. This could mean destitution, especially if they had a family, unless they could find another job without a reference. They only had the workhouse to fall back on, where husbands and wives were separated and the title, 'workhouse', meant what it said with a vengeance. If the man was single, he might join the rank of the numerous tramps who literally tramped the countryside and slept in barns.

Mr. Thompson's authority extended to the labourers' children, who were obliged to wear the clothes that he provided for them under the guise of benevolence. The boys were all dressed in grey and the girls in black frocks with white starched aprons with frilly epaulettes – no doubt preparing them for 'service', which was to be the lot of the girls.

Mr. Thompson was succeeded by his cousin Mr. Parsons, also a banker, and he continued the rule of authority, although there is no evidence that he made use of the bedroom mirror. He lived at the Manor with his sister, who had a much more benign view of her role as lady of the Manor. Her brother was more inclined to preserve the law and order of the village through his taskmaster, a Mr. Hill, a corpulent figure, who rode round the village on his horse looking for troublemakers. He had previously been employed by Mr. Thompson and was able to continue the rod of iron. His speciality was to hunt down the boys who were scrumping up the fruit trees in the autumn. When he caught the boys pinching fruit, apples or pears, he would use his horsewhip on their unprotected legs; they were easy targets up in the trees at just the right height to whip them from his horse. If they did escape, he would get permission to search them out in the school playground, but no-one would split on them although everyone knew who the culprits were.

But this brutality was finally stopped: he once went too far when Jimmy Maltby went home covered with weals from the horsewhip. The next day his mother was looking out for Mr Hill and according to Jimmy's story, "When he came trotting down the road – plonk, plonk, plonk – she got hold of one of his legs and pulled him off onto the hard ground. He was a fat old chap and landed on the ground with a resounding thump… he was a devil." Apparently there does not seem to be any record of repercussions: he was probably afraid of an enquiry into his brutality towards the boys.

But the best aspects of the feudal system were well preserved by Miss Parsons when she moved from the Manor to Home Farm, living alone after the death of her brother who, according to the village, died a millionaire. Home Farm was in fact the original Manor. It had long low Georgian windows almost reaching to the ground, with impeccable lawns descending from them, ablaze with daffodils in spring. She was the last of the Parsons, but the Thompsons were still going strong at Woodperry in a beautiful house, where she was fetched by car every Sunday to have lunch with them. She was well respected by all of the villagers and we were kept informed of various details of her privileged life through her two servants: Mrs Huxley, the enormous cook, and the maid who was also quite plump. There were little details of her day to day life, for instance, the time when she tasted brains on toast from the brawn made out of the pig's head and enjoyed them; but what caught our imagination was the time when she actually had her operation for appendicitis at home! She was a figure of another age and we children thought that she was extremely old although she was probably only in her fifties.

She devoted a great deal of her time to the well-being of the villagers. She was a familiar figure on Monday afternoons calling at every house in the village. She was always dressed the same: grey costume of the early twenties, with the tapered jacket coming well down over the long skirt; white lace blouse tight across the neck, with an oval jet brooch fastening it. Her only protection against the weather was a black hat securely fastened with jet hatpins over her snow-white hair, gathered in a tight bun under it.

For the farm labourers, she had a system of saving: the coal club and the shoe club and she carried all their cards in a little cloth bag noting down each week how much they were able to put aside for these two essential items. Then the day after Boxing Day, they could claim their savings and not be tempted to spend it injudiciously for Christmas. As the Warner children had to wait

John Buchan
with his children:
Alice, Billie,
Alistair and
Johnny.

for the money for the Christmas treat, this meant seeing the Christmas decorations being pulled down instead of in all their glory. But they were always philosophical and Did said that she did not mind too much. Later when Miss Parsons became more frail, Miss Stace took over the savings clubs.

We could more or less tell the time by Miss Parsons' knock on the front door at four o'clock on a Monday afternoon; during my childhood I do not recall that she ever missed a week. For us it was war savings: a sixpenny stamp for Monty and one for me. I could not help wondering why we were saving for war, since it was over. I learnt later that it was instituted during the First World War and had continued – presumably in advance for the Second. I literally took advantage of this as when I was finding the pinch during the Second World War, I suddenly remembered Miss Parsons and my old books of savings stored away in the dresser and I took some pleasure in cashing the lot.

If there was a special need, Miss Parsons would meet it. She provided the means for Perp Newell, the hunchback, to have training in a cobbler's trade; he grumbled a lot about it, but it did provide him with a living, which would have been difficult otherwise. She also obtained training in basketry for Hugh Pinker who was practically blind. There is more about her benevolence in the account of Christmas and Easter and also in my needlework lessons. She was well respected by everyone and lived to be a hundred, dying on Christmas Day, which was also the day of her birth.

So it was the end of an era when in 1921 Mr. Parsons sold the whole village to Christ Church College, Oxford and a new lord came to occupy the Manor House who fulfilled his role with courtesy and consideration. This was John Buchan, the writer. The whole Buchan family made themselves an integral part of the community and went to great lengths to play an active part in the village life. Mrs. Buchan was president of the Women's Institute and the meetings had a special aura, being held in the august Manor drawing room. This was also the venue for the thriving amateur dramatic society, which had such success in the county competitions.

Mr. Buchan was a familiar figure riding round the countryside on his beautiful bay horse, always passing the time with the villagers, who had nothing to fear from his ascendancy. He would attend church every Sunday in the very front pew with his wife and his family of four and the word went round, as did every word in the village, that he appreciated the vicar's sermons and Mr Ellkington made great efforts to be worthy of such high praise. I did not share this view; my thoughts were entirely occupied in wondering when it would end.

The eldest son, Johnny, was a practised falconer and wherever he went he had his tame falcon on his shoulder.

The Buchans carried out their obligations to the village as a sort of benign presence and their largesse reached its zenith in the festive seasons, Christmas and Easter, with none of the imposition of uniform for the children as in previous times. But it was all the year round that their obvious appreciation of the Oxfordshire countryside made a bond between us, even if the still rigid class system meant that we did not share it on an equal footing. We had no idea, for instance, that the motorbike often seen outside the Manor actually belonged to the famous Lawrence of Arabia; in any case we had never heard of him.

The Church

The church played a great part in our lives from birth to death. It is a modest building, boasting neither spire nor tower, but its very simplicity matched our lives.

In the Oxfordshire archives however it is described as follows, "One of the prettiest Church Yards was Elsfield with its nicely kept Roses all down the Fence separating the path from the Yard." It goes on, "The Clerk, Mr Basson, rang the bells and said the responses in Church very loud, his singing to lead the congregation." Most villagers went to church at least once a Sunday, often in the evening so that it did not encroach on the established ritual of the Sunday dinner.

But it was only a generation ago that, for many people in the village, whether girls in service or farm labourers, church attendance was more or less compulsory. Even when young girls in service had their Sunday off, the church services dominated their hours. It was usually a 'full' day off every other Sunday, from after washing up the breakfast things until the evensong at 6 o'clock, and the alternate half-day was after the Sunday lunch washing up – always a prolonged affair – until the same evensong. This meant that it was difficult to walk to their home and back in the time. "If you didn't return in time for the six o'clock service you were asked why. You had to tell them a story – no way of getting out of it. Yes, most of the village had to go; church used to be full up there on a Sunday."

Old men would recall similar unwritten regulations: as farm labourers they were duty bound to go to church at least once on a Sunday. However after the old Lord of the Manor left, it just fell through. Certainly the farmers I knew when I was young would not have dreamt of such domination. My father was not a regular church attender himself; although he always went to the harvest festival, saying ruefully, "You might sing, 'All is safely gathered in' but that isn't you know; it's still in rows wet through." Nevertheless the church had a considerable influence on all our lives: in spite of erstwhile compulsions, most of us regarded it as natural to attend regularly.

In my case I was expected to attend morning service from my earliest years, sitting in our pew, which was behind Mr. Hatt's, which was behind John Buchan's. Farmers had pews allocated according to the acreage they rented. I didn't understand what Mr. Elkington was saying in his sermon, but I was duly impressed by this awe-inspiring white robed figure who denounced the ungodly with such passionate eloquence. I learnt to welcome the words, "And now to God the Father...," which meant that it was over at long last. When the plate was handed round, I really surmised that I was being rewarded for having sat through this long harangue so quietly and I helped myself to as

Elsfield Church: the altar and pews. Our pew was the third on the right, behind John Buchan and Mr Hatt.

many coins as my little fists would hold and proceeded to the door with a feeling that it had been worthwhile after all. But alas! they caught up with me by the time I reached the porch and I was peremptorily relieved of my ill-gained spoil!

Sunday School was more appropriate to my age group, although I was still greatly mystified by the procedures, at least to begin with. We would come early on Sunday afternoons to explore the churchyard and the older girls literally put the fear of God into me saying I was walking on the dead. You were never supposed to walk on a grave and, as almost everywhere I could put my foot down there was a hidden mound covering a nameless corpse, they could make a strong case. I soon learnt to wedge my little shoes in the grooves between and read with awe the words engraved on the tombstones, particularly of those who had died young. The ancient stones were often covered with lichen and moss, which we delighted in scratching off.

Sunday School was conducted by a benevolent young man, son of the farmer living opposite the church. He was Mervyn Hatt, but always called Sandy, on account of his already thinning auburn hair. He later became a missionary and sadly was murdered in India. He was gentle with us, although his idea of finding texts of a sequence of words, starting with one word then two and presumably onto eternity, was a difficult task. He gave us one example, 'God is Love', for number three; any others were completely beyond me and I did rather feel that he had 'collared the market' (as we would say now), as it was the only one I knew. Much later he visited us at our new farm and gave me a welcome hand with my Latin homework, which gave me an insight into the poetry of Virgil that I had never appreciated before.

I have to confess that my chief pleasure in attending Sunday School was to be able to show off my Sunday best white frock, trimmed with lace or broderie anglaise, and my cloche straw hat, trimmed with artificial flowers or cherries. The dresses always had a series of wide tucks so that they could last a few years of growth; this gave them a sort of ballerina appearance, which I tried to use to my advantage.

The Sunday School girls (I do not recall any boys) were promoted to sing as a choir behind the harmonium, played energetically by Miss Cox or Mrs. Webb and sometimes by my mother, and I always looked forward to singing the hymns with all the lustiness my voice could command. The words presented some problems however, "There is a green hill far away, without a city wall." I thought that it would be far more unusual and worthy of comment to have a green hill with its city wall and I pictured a huge luscious mound with a city wall encircling it as an alternative. I was already beginning to query what was laid before me as gospel.

Some of the service, that we repeated until we knew it by heart, puzzled me as to its meaning. There was one passage in particular where I always repeated, "The earth and all the anemones," and I couldn't for the life of me see why they had been singled out as a source of wonder. It is true that they were growing in their thousands in all the woods nearby in springtime, casting a haze of pure white above their feathery leaves. At school I learnt about colourful anemones that swam in the ocean. Were they the ones? Only when I was quite a bit older did I realise that the passage ran, "the earth, the sea and all that in them is" and therefore covering the whole planet.

Many of the more military hymns we had learnt at school, with the boys in full throttle, 'Fight the good fight' and 'Onward Christian soldiers'. But there was one particular hymn, that we only sang in church, that made me feel sad and overwhelmed. It was, 'Oh God our help in ages past', with the lines, 'A thousand ages in thy sight, Are like an evening gone' and again 'Time like an ever-rolling stream, Bears all its sons away; They fly forgotten like a-dream, Flies at the opening day'. This hymn was associated in my mind with the sudden death of Mrs. Brown, mother to Molly who was my age. This early intimation of my mortality was hard to bear, or rather it was the idea of my parents 'flying away forgotten' that seemed to spark off a sadness which often made me heavy-hearted and depressed for no apparent reason.

Was it the Day of Judgment that hung over me like the sword of Damocles? I knew exactly the sort of weather that would herald this awe-inspiring event: the sky would be turbulent, the clouds dark and menacing, racing at speed across the heavens. If it was combined with a lurid, blood-red sunset haunting behind the billowing thunderclouds, then I felt that the chances of the world coming to an abrupt end were even stronger. My fears were not centred on my immediate destiny to hell, although I had little doubt that that would be my lot, it was the shame of all the people in the village knowing how bad I was that haunted me.

I attended church regularly until I was confirmed and I never questioned its inevitability: everyone had to be confirmed. There were several weeks of preparation with the Reverend Elkington, but what transpired during these attendances remains a complete blank to me. I recall having a white dress, specially made, which I later tried to shorten into a tennis frock with unforeseen results. It was more like an early edition of the mini, as I had cut it into an almost everlasting spiral! Mr. Brown, the farmer from Sescut, was summoned at the last minute to be my godfather, standing in for my father, who was coping with the birth of a foal in a breach position. As was the custom, he presented me with a prayer book; it was rather elegant with shiny ivory covers. However as I grew towards adolescence these concerns took a back place in my mind and only later did I begin to realise the value of the religious background that I had experienced at an early age.

There was a lot of voluntary work given to the church, which was always in need of help and few funds to pay for it. There were the bells to ring and the organ to blow on Sundays and, when Bessie Phipps was asked to do both, she felt that she couldn't refuse, "If you said 'no' you would have to have a good excuse as they would ask, 'Why can't you?'" But she did add, "People did that out of friendship." During the war she even took on the job of gravedigger, as there was no-one else to do it.

The solemnity of grave digging was sometimes tempered with a sense of humour and my father's graveyard stories were part of a tradition of village folklore. The gravedigger in the next village, Beckley, for example, was quite a wag. Because of the over-crowded nature of ancient churchyards, he often dug up the bones and skulls of previous occupants and he would put a lighted candle in a skull and place it on top of the pile of earth and this used to frighten the children as they passed by on their way to school. If he unearthed a more recent coffin, he would lift the lid and shake hands with the skeleton, with appropriate speech, such as, "Hello George. I didn't think I would see you again, after all these years." Once he discovered several skeletons laid side by side, with one at the others' feet. Was it a military burial, possibly from the time of the Civil War? There had been much skirmishing in the Beckley-Islip area. Or was it a result of bubonic plague or typhus, which were prevalent in both areas at that time? But Elsfield's graveyard did not reveal any such secrets.

If anyone died, there would always be a volunteer to toll the bell, once for every year of their life. So the ninety-year-olds, and there were some, had ninety tolls. It gave a shiver down my back whenever I heard it and we all knew who it was and what had happened; death made an awesome impression on us children.

For the funeral, they used to carry the coffin, as there was no hearse. There would be six strong chaps and if it was from the other end of the village and the dead man was heavy, "That was a long way." They would sometimes use a cart and, out of respect for the dead, they would strew straw on the road to deaden the noise of the cartwheels.

Sunday was a day of rest. Apart from church attendance, there were family traditions, such as the walk together on Sunday evenings in summer and singing round the piano in the winter. There were also quite a few restrictions according to individuals' beliefs. We did no sewing on Sundays, but knitting was permitted, and knowing how seamstresses worked their fingers to the bone in Victorian times, one can understand the origin of these restrictions. In my opinion, some people went too far, as when play with balls and skipping was frowned upon. But these were now remnants of a past age.

Before leaving the church, I must pay a special tribute to Reverend Elkington. He provided a link between the formality of worship and our everyday life. He was a cheery soul and we called him Daddy Elkington. He would often be seem making his way over the fields to the White Horse pub at Headington and back, and this seemed to be a bond with the village folk. They would say, "He likes his drop of tiddly." The boys had good memories of his generosity. "When we went to Marston on foot to catch the bus to go to Oxford for carpentry, we used to meet him on the way back and, before we got to him, he would be looking in his pockets and, when we got up to him, he would throw out some coins on the road for us to scramble over. He was a good old chap."

There was another earlier connection between the church and the Manor. This was when Mrs. Parsons, the lady of the Manor, funded a reredos in the chancel, depicting the Lord's Supper. The money to pay for it was saved by making butter at the Manor dairy and then the skim milk was given out to the villagers at 8 am every morning. When I heard this account of what happened before my time, I thought that it seemed like giving the villagers an example of thrift and getting up early in the morning.

Mrs Hambidge's shop and post office in the 1930s. © Oxfordshire County Council Photographic Archive.

The Shop

According to the scanty archives, an old lady, Sarah Clay, ran the first shop in the village. She had a small cottage in the middle of the village and in her window were bottles of sweets and under the counter she kept tobacco, which would need a licence if declared. Each Saturday she could be seen, with her apron over her frock and a basket on each arm, trudging down the road to get her supplies from Oxford.

After her death, a Mr. Saunders took over in a cottage which was in ruins by my time and was a source of endless precarious games for us, as it was quite dangerous and falling apart. Besides the sweets and illicit tobacco, he would sell the Blenheim apples and conference pears at a penny a pound – fruits that I later enjoyed for free. A few years later, a Mrs. Webb took over, adding mineral waters to her repertoire. Finally, someone I knew, Mrs. Allam, when she became widowed, went to run the shop with her daughter, Mrs. Dennis. Their cottage became my favourite spot in the whole village. I had a penny a week pocket money and for that I could get two varieties, all at a halfpenny each: a braid of liquorice, which broke into strings called shoelaces; everlasting toffee, called 'Waggle, waggle'; gob-stoppers, which revealed a flat surface with rings of all different colours when you rubbed them on a wall; pale pink shrimps; white and pint fondant mice with white wick tails; sherbet dabs and a marshmallow with a trinket inside. With such choice there was much deliberation involved and old Mrs. Allam was never in a hurry. I could also of course blue all my money on five butterballs for a penny.

When she died, I grieved – partly for her who was a real friend and partly for an absence of sweets. My mother suggested that I should pick a bunch of

violets, which she loved, to put on her grave alongside the wreaths and bouquets, but I was too shy, feeling that my little offering would be insignificant

My abstinence was short-lived as Mrs. Hambidge branched out on a much more lavish shop and later on a post office. My speciality there was cherry cider in a bottle with a ball stopper inside. I saw one recently in an antique shop marked at a high price, but in those days, after paying our three pence, we would always return them to the shop. Some time later we managed to buy a packet of Woodbines, after asking in a theatrical voice, "What did Monty want?" The experience that followed in the depths of Woodeaton wood was nauseous and put me off smoking for the rest of my life.

Chapter 6

The Villagers

The rich variety of villagers combined to make a pulsating community, all interacting, yet each family with a different role in the hierarchy, which was for the most part benevolently structured. It is true that we were all aware of our place in the class system, but this did not prevent us from knowing that we were an essential part of an integrated whole. Without this spirit, Elsfield would have been just a row of houses along a winding street, which is what it seems to be now.

The Farmers

In the hierarchy of power, after the Manor and the church, came the farmers. There were three farms in the village and another down the fields near the river Cherwell, at Sescut. Mr. Watts rented the largest number of fields at one end of the village and my father farmed on a much smaller scale at the other. In between was Mr. Hatt, who must have had a private income, as he seemed to leave all the actual farm work to his men. All the farming land now belonged to Christ Church College and as far as we were concerned, as the least affluent, there was always a financial crisis at the time of the rent audit twice a year. Somehow my father always managed to raise the money, but with great anxiety beforehand, which I shared but felt powerless to help. I thought at least he had a good dinner in the Christ Church hall. Times were hard for farmers between the two World Wars and of course even harder for the precariously employed farm labourers.

Mr. Watts

Mr. Watts probably carried the same anxiety about money and he had good reason; after his death his son, Freddie, who took over the farm, went bankrupt, which was a great disgrace in those days. Village opinion was not divided on his ability to shout, "He used to shout right up the village; he was a powerful bloke," and again, "Really the way he used to shout – we could hear him shouting, 'Come on you beggars'." Because of his religion,

Hill Farm where the Watts family lived.

Methodist, he would never swear, but he made the expression, "It's a beggar-rooter of a job" more explosive than its profane counterpart. Mr Watts was alright, according to Jimmy Maltby, but he liked everything to be done, no slacking. He always thought he was right, but when Jimmy told him that to his face he used to get so angry that he threw his hat on the ground. When he was in a bad mood, or beside himself with anger, some of his six daughters were commandeered to sing to him to cure his headache.

The Watts were strictly chapel and the whole family, all eight of them, piled into the elderly but spacious car to worship at the Methodist chapel in Pembroke Street every Sunday morning. There was always a feeling of confrontation between church and chapel in the village, with the great majority being 'church'; in fact the Watts were the sole representatives of 'chapel'. These differences came to a head over a particularly prolific walnut tree, which was paradoxically growing in the Watts's field, but in the area that was allocated to the church according to ancient glebe land rights. We children had no idea of the reasons for this disputed ownership, but we certainly profited by the confusion and assumed that the prized walnuts were a free-for-all. We invaded the field with sticks and stones to knock them down and came home loaded with them still in their green husks. Replete with the delicious tang of sweet walnuts, we had to spend the evening scrubbing our hands to get rid of the stains.

Later on I heard that they had resolved their feud. Geraldine Elkington, the vicar's daughter, had the walnut tree fenced round and then Mr. Watts went to Christ Church, the landlords, to have it formally divided. His part was then fenced off and the vicar had to keep his half clean from weeds. That was after my time of walnut 'scrumping', but I'm sure the children still climbed over the two fences, as they would still believe that the walnuts were theirs for the picking. I thought, at the time, that share and share alike was much better than fighting, but I was happy to profit by the controversy over ownership.

Mr. Hatt

Mr. Hatt, who was known not unkindly as 'Old Johnnie Bonnet', was 'posh'. His accent confirmed that, although his favourite expression was "Yo," which punctuated all of his conversation and his listening. The other proof of being posh was that they had late dinner, according to Eileen Hambidge, who was in service there. His wife was a complete cripple from arthritis and spent her time in an armchair looking out on to the village street. He was a familiar figure on horseback, in full riding gear and a bowler hat, riding leisurely through the village.

May and Herbie Allam

May Allam was a stalwart of the village; it seemed to revolve round her, probably because she was unofficially in charge of the village notice board. This was in the form of a huge truncated elm, studded with tacks and drawing pins and announcements, and situated just outside her cottage opposite the Manor. In her youth, she taught as an assistant in the village school and left to look after her consumptive husband, Herbie, who was struggling as a carpenter, which he ployed in the Buchan's barn opposite their cottage. The flying sawdust must have had a detrimental effect on his health, although the wide doors were always kept open in lieu of windows. He sported a rather jaunty boater over his thinning hair and white, almost translucent, complexion; he was as thin as a rake and when I saw him with his amply proportioned wife, I could not help thinking of Jack Sprat.

In spite of his obvious illness, I was really envious of him on two counts. He slept in a little wooden summerhouse in his garden with door and windows open to benefit from the open air, and to me this was sheer magic. Also, he was the first one in the village to get a crystal set and, by manipulating the delicate instrument called the cat's whisker, he could get a faint rendering of music or talk. I was drawn to his hut as a bee to honey, as soon as he came home from the barn. I gathered that the Buchans had helped him with the wooden hut and had presented him with the crystal set.

May and Herbie Allaum's cottage.

To return to his devoted wife, May; she was a fulsome woman with upright carriage and hair swept in a generous bun. When I knew her she was always dressed in black, long before her husband died. Her voluminous skirt, which nearly reached her ankles, was covered with an equally ample black apron and above was a black high-necked blouse, clasped with a jet brooch and, on chilly days, a black triangular shawl draped her shoulders. She represented the previous generation, who had usually taken to wearing black in their later years, which was probably in their fifties; but like them, she braved her arthritis with the aid of a stick and went about the village business with endless energy.

John Buchan wrote a whole book about Jack Allam, Mrs. Allam's brother, and his work entitled, 'Always a Countryman'. It gives a graphic picture of the gamekeeper, who would always be carrying a couple of pheasants or a brace of rabbits. He married three times, as two former wives died. (I don't think we knew the meaning of the word 'divorce'). He loved children, but had none of his own, and always had a cheery word for us as he traipsed through the village. The son of his third wife, Frank Sharp, was the only Elsfield casualty of the Second World War and he was killed in Canada.

The village business was unending for May Allam. She was always making the clothes donated by order of the lord of the Manor and later she continued her role as village dressmaker for the Buchan family. She made

Alice Buchan's wedding dress and also the dress in which Alice was presented at court and jokingly said that she could therefore be considered as court dressmaker. She always did the cricket teas and we used to hang around to get any leftovers, they were so good. She was the secretary of the Women Institute and also contributed to the village archives, for which I am really grateful.

Mr Paintin, Mr Warner and the two Wingfield brothers.

The Warner Family

Before he came to Elsfield to follow Mr. Watts, Mr. Warner had had a chequered history. His grandfather had been a gentleman farmer and quite well-to-do, but unfortunately, soon after his death, Mr. Warner and his brothers and sisters became orphans and were placed in the not-so-tender care of their aunt. Apparently she was a 'dreadful woman'; she was very strict and insisted on them wearing navy blue suits or dresses and always kid gloves. If they even looked at anyone when they were with her, she would box their ears. So childhood was far from easy, although they must have had some compensation in having donkeys to ride to school every day! When I heard this story I wondered if they still had to wear the kid gloves when riding, which would have got very dirty.

After leaving school at thirteen, Mr. Warner broke away from this authoritarian household and got a number of part-time jobs: first an apprenticeship

The Warner girls, 1926. Did is top right.

at a draper's, then working for his brother in a butcher's shop. He had a major change of direction when, after courting a lady's maid for seven years, she said, "What's the use of marrying you? You haven't got a regular income" and that's why he decided to become a farm worker and why they landed up at Elsfield with Mr Watts some years later.

The journey to Enfield was quite traumatic, as Mr. Watts had insisted that the family, which by now comprised three girls and another child due in a fortnight, shared the small pony and trap with two calves! Mrs. Warner protested, "Supposing anybody sees us – going right through Oxford with two calves!" Mr Warner assured her that no-one knew them at Oxford, but, sure enough, as they were driving over Carfax, a voice came from nowhere, "Hello Sid! What are you doing with those calves?" Mrs. Warner was mortified.

There was always a continual struggle to make ends meet, especially now with five girls to feed. However Mrs. Warner worked wonders; she made all the girls' dresses and, as they were always so well turned out, they never qualified for the attractive handouts of clothes that the Manor bestowed on some families, whose children went about like ragamuffins or, as Did Warner put it, 'scruffy'. It was also galling that the wealthy aunt bequeathed her entire worldly goods, house and furniture to Mr. Warner's sister and he received nothing.

But they were all very resourceful. Mrs. Warner would make nets out of string to cook the vegetables in one saucepan, adding them according to the time they needed. This was just one example of the way she economised so that they were always provided with good nourishing food. The girls were also fully co-operative: they would never think of going for a walk, long or short, without coming back laden with wood for the range. To give an example of their resourcefulness, there was a place in Beckley, a village over a mile away, where in the autumn they sold Victoria plums for a penny a pound. They would set off on their father's bike with Aggie peddling with her legs underneath the bar and Did standing up on the back all the way. They always managed to bring back ten pounds of plums and two of dough for their mother to make dough cakes filled with plums.

Did earned three pence a week for delivering milk to Miss Parsons every day except Sundays; she had first to call for the empty can, get the milk from the farm and then deliver it. For her pains she was also rewarded with a pair of green glass vases that Miss Parsons said she had had on her mantelpiece for fifty years. Many years later they turned out to be quite valuable antiques, which was quite a bonus and there were many such treasures hidden away in the cottages as well as with the gentry.

Although she had to leave school at the age of eleven, or perhaps because of that, Mrs. Warner was a great reader. In those days you could leave the village school if you passed the fourth standard, which was generally obtained at the age of thirteen. She was allowed to leave early, as she was proficient in the three Rs at the age of twelve, and then she worked in wonderful establishments as a lady's maid until she was married at thirty. She would often read the newspaper or a book to her husband, when he came home at night too tired to read himself. She found that it was best to wait for the morning before broaching the question of money for extra household needs. When he was tired out, she would get the stock response that all the women seemed to get, "You must think money grows on trees."

Jimmy Maltby

Jimmy Maltby was quite a bit older than me and I got his story and his forthright comments when he was eighty. I always remembered him in the village because of his hare lip, which, although he had an operation straight away when he was born, it was not possible to eradicate, as it would be today.

According to Jimmy, he was naughty as a child and went to live with his grandmother who lived just down the road. She made a great fuss of him, piling on the food but being cautious enough to fill him up with good solid suet pudding first, so that he didn't need so much meat! This happy state of affairs was brought to an abrupt end when he was seven, when his grandfather died and the tied cottage was wanted for another worker. His grandmother had to move to Oxford and he never saw her again.

When he was five or six, he and his brother were sent to their other Grandpa during the First World War. It couldn't have been for safety as there were Zeppelins over London; he didn't know why. In any case, the stay only lasted six weeks that were miserable for Jimmy. He went to school there and the children poked fun at him as a country bumpkin. His brother was in a gang who were streetwise and they were adept at pinching from stores and running off. Jimmy could not run so fast and lagged behind and of course got caught. He was so happy to go back in the train to the other grandparents who spoiled him.

At Elsfield, he led the life of the other boys, bird's nesting, and was often chased by the keepers so that the 'game' was not disturbed, as the lord of the Manor had all the shooting rights of pheasants and partridges. Rabbiting was the prerogative of the farmers.

By the age of eight, Jimmy had started milking and was working all weekend 'doing' the chickens and tending to the family pig. As soon as he had left school at just fourteen, he was doing a full-time farm worker's job. That meant he had to wake up at 4.30 am and work until 5 pm with some evenings thrown in and with time off on Sundays only between milking. The cows had to be milked night and morning, weekdays and weekends alike.

His confrontation with the foreman of the lord of the Manor has already been told and this is just one example of the remnants of the feudal system. Jimmy was an outstanding example of someone who would be courageous enough to stand up for his own rights.

Pets

Everybody had at least one pet and often several. Their diet was a natural one as the dogs caught rats and the cats caught mice. This was supplemented with plenty of scraps; the pet food industry had not reached us. Pets were considered as bone fide members of their family; each animal was given the respect of having the surname of its owner, so it was always Rex Webb or Spider Buchan. Spider was what they called 'a bit of a monkey', although he was designated as a toy dog; he was a mass of long white hair with a black patch over each eye, probably partly a Sealyham. When he died, we all knew that he had been given a real funeral and had been buried in Mrs. Buchan's silk scarf.

Rex Webb was a source of fear to me and when I went past he came out chasing me with a sharp terrier bark, which made me run for dear life, which encouraged him to give chase. His housemate was Ginger Webb, a doctored sandy male cat with a white beard and a complete contrast with his lethargic tranquillity.

Rover and Bing Allam were black and liver-and-white retrievers respectively; they were always to be seen outside Mrs Allam's cottage that faced the village notice board tree, which had lived to such a good age that it was no more than a huge hollow trunk. Paintin's dog was a cross-breed, but a sheepdog at heart and could be found following Mr. Watts's sheep wherever they had been driven.

The pets rarely got lost and if they strayed they were soon restored to their owners. Sidney Webb even found a tiny kitten in a ditch on a wet night as he was cycling home; he put it in his vest and it was found that it belonged to the Hatt's and Eileen Hatt was delighted to find that it had not been drowned. Pets roamed freely in the village, just as we did, as there was no danger of being run over by the traffic, which was almost non-existent.

Service

Just as the boys went into full-time farm work the moment they left school, so the girls in the farm workers' homes went into service. Jimmy Maltby's wife described her life from the age of fourteen in service at Noke, a small village about four miles from Elsfield. The girls had all been well versed in household chores from an early age, but this life was much more demanding. In her own words, "Oh. It was horrible!" They would have to get up at six to light the range and prepare breakfast and then do all the usual chores: the washing up, emptying the 'slops', airing and then making the beds, preparing the vegetables, serving at lunch, tea and dinner, and washing up, as well as all the washing and ironing. There were also seasonal jobs, like lighting the old combustion boiler in the church in winter.

Break time was one half day a week plus every other Sunday, which was only after washing up the midday lunch and being back at half past nine and not a minute later. On the other Sunday there was only a short break, after washing up the tea things until bedtime. But even these Sunday breaks were compulsorily controlled, as it was expected that the maids would attend Evensong, as they obviously hadn't the possibility of taking time off for Matins on Sunday morning. This meant that it was impossible to walk to the village where their family lived, in spite of the Sunday 'half day'. Some households were less exacting towards their maids and on the long Sundays they could go home for a few hours, but on the short Sundays they still had to go to church.

In retrospect, what Mrs. Maltby hated most was the uniform: the mob cap and large white apron in the morning and little apron and frilly cap in the afternoon, always with a black dress, thick black woollen stockings and equally heavy black shoes. She realised how much she had to accept, "We never had to mind in those days, we didn't take much notice of it then, but they wouldn't do it today."

It is interesting to hear about Mrs. Maltby's life in the village before she had to go into service. "It was a lovely life really, but there was no play after school. We had to go down to the woods to collect wood for the next day and break it up for mother to use it in the morning, Then there was the mending and ironing and by that time it was time to go to bed. Now it's all rush and go, isn't it? But then you could take your time and there was nothing to rush back for. In the winter evenings, we used to sit and make rag rugs, not to sell, but as there were no carpets, they covered the board or stone floors."

Before going into service, she was already working on Saturday mornings; she went to clean up for a family and was rewarded with two thick slices of bread with apricot jam and half-a-crown. Then she would have to hurry back to get her dad's dinner, as her mother had to go to Oxford by carrier's cart to do the week's shopping.

Opportunities for Change

But the twenties were giving way to the thirties and both boys and girls began to have some choice and our generation was already spreading its wings. This was in contrast to the old villager, who said to my father that he had only once been to foreign parts. My father thought that it must have been during the war, although most farm labourers were in the reserved category, but in fact it was only to Banbury about fifteen miles away! Young men were becoming aware that there were jobs in the car industry, like Morris Motors and what they called the Steel Press. Lord Nuffield of Morris cars, previously Sir William Morris, was quite a lowly native of Oxford and my father recalled with some relish that 'Old Billie Morris' used to come round to mend his punctures for a few pence! But that was long ago. He finally became one of the biggest magnates in the car industry and when the élite village of Nuffield allegedly rejected him as a member of their golf club, he bought it up lock, stock and barrel and took the name as his title as a lord.

There was also the opening of the milk round; this was probably the beginning of that essentially English custom to have the milk delivered. It had always been the job of the tenant farmers' wives or their daily helps to serve milk at the back door for the villagers who came in the early morning to have their jugs filled. As I got older, I was given the task of measuring out the pints and the quarts from the churn to their jugs, which was a meaningful lesson in 'capacity'. But this was all to change, with possible alternatives to farm labouring such as the milk round. One example was in neighbouring Beckley; the surrounding villages had no milk delivery service and so, instead of taking the milk to Oxford on a wholesale basis, the Wheeler family started a retail milk round in 2½ gallon buckets, measuring the milk into customers' jugs with either a pint or half pint measure. The milk was sold at 2½d (a fraction over 1p) a pint and then they branched out into eggs at 6d (2½p) a dozen.

With such possible alternatives to farm labouring, workers could be more defiant to their bosses, as illustrated by the case of Harold Wingfield: he was under-carter to Mr. Watts, who ordered him not to put the horses overnight in a field that saved Harold a lot of walking. Messages were exchanged. "You've got to get the horses out of that field. They shouldn't be in there!" from Mr. Watts, who was nothing if not choleric. Harold's reply came back via the student farmer, "You go back and tell Mr. Watts, if he wants them he can move them." In the morning, when he was looking after his horses, out came Mr. Watts and gave him the sack. He was married and had two children and had to leave his tied cottage. But fortunately he 'did very well for himself', getting employment in an extensive milk round. Previously the threat of the family being turned out would scare them into complete submission.

The girls began to have similar escape options, as opposed to going into service, when they left school. For example, Did Warner served her time of apprenticeship in millinery at Oxford's most exclusive drapers, Ellistons. This was no easy option as Did, Cathie to them, described. The interview was presided over by a very 'snooty' buyer, who indicated that she was doing them a great service. Did and her elder sister, Hilda, had cycled to Oxford in the pouring rain and she agreed that they did look a couple of 'ikes', dripping wet. She was graciously accepted however and started the following Saturday with her compulsory black dress with white collar provided. The apprentices were the ones who really did great service; they were paid 4s 5d a week during three years, working from 8.30 in the morning until 6 at night with just a half day on Thursdays. After that she received 32 shillings a week during the nine years she served. Miss Fawcett, her supervisor, was very hard and strict and would inform her, "You're too slow, Miss Warner, I'll have send a note to your father." No encouragement was given: they always said you were no good.

There was also Mildred Dennis, granddaughter of old Mrs Allam who kept the small village shop; she branched out into working in an electrical shop. There were also opportunities for girls to work daily for women dons at Oxford colleges: Audrey Phipps worked daily at St Hilda's for six years and then privately for Miss Taylor, a don at Christ Church. Although hard work, this was not to be compared with the servitude of 'service'.

Visitors to the Village

There was a constant stream of traders to the village, who were called by the day they came, like the 'Thursday man'. He was a baker and he was actually called Baker, so he was also known as 'Baker Baker'. His speciality was fatty cakes and he was so proud of them that when he pronounced the word 'fatty' it was as if he was salivating over them and indeed they were delicious. When we took a bite, the butter would ooze out over our chins. He went down in the annals of Elsfield for having walked from Beckley across the fields with two great big baskets of bread when the snow was up to the hedge tops. There was enough for each family to have one loaf each at 4½d.

But Mr. Baker Baker's loaves, though so welcome to the snowed-up villagers, were steam cooked whereas Mr. Gatz's were baked in a proper oven. Mr Gatz was of German origin, having settled in Beckley before the First World War and, although there was some anti-German feeling during and after the war, there seemed to be no prejudice against him personally. In fact he was as popular as his loaves, which were crisp and warm when he delivered them in his huge square basket and we would creep into the pantry the moment he left and tear off great crusts from the cottage loaves or, at times of hunger, the whole topknot. My mother would smile indulgently as we would offer explanations about mice.

Mr Gatz was a jolly fellow with very fair hair; he came regularly three times a week in his pony and trap, often accompanied by his equally fair-haired sons. The all had blue eyes as well and would presumably have been welcome citizens of Hitler's Reich in the thirties. He also ran the sole taxi service for miles around.

Equally jolly was the postman, Billie, always with a smile, a regular 'rat tat tat' on the front door, with the greeting, "Hello Monty, hello Mildred." He knew the names of all the villagers down to the youngest babies. Afterwards I learnt that his young daughter had died during this time, yet he was always so cheerful.

The coalman was another regular; he came every Saturday morning, his carthorse dragging the trailer full of sacks of coal, straining every muscle up Elsfield hill. A sack of coal was two shillings, but if they could get hold of a horse and cart, the villagers used to take it to Oxford and buy a whole ton much cheaper. It was sold in great boulders, which had to be broken down and stored, with all the family helping with various versions of coal hammers. The coalman was appropriately called 'Mr Carter', his real name, and once he gave us a lift in his 'coal cart', which was like a wagon without any sides. We got filthy and it was hard work not to be jogged off the edge.

The sweep used to come regularly for years; he used to walk from Headington across the fields. He would do all the chimneys at the Manor before any of the village cottages; so it was really late before he could wend his way back carrying all of his brushes.

There was also a nice old man from North Oxford, who came once a month selling Scripture Union cards for pennies and cut-price Bibles at a shilling. He would bring text cards and little calendars and a publication called 'Our Own Magazine' with serials that continued from month to month, so he was always eagerly awaited for us children to read what happened next. His impact was considerable and some of the children who joined the Scripture Union have been members ever since.

Then there were numbers of semi-regulars: as for example, 'Old Scarlet', the rag-and-bone man who would come on a rackety old bike to collect old rubbish and bring a big sack round to fill it. He would always say "Got anything to sell today?" and Did Warner remembers how she was frightened to death when her father would reply, "Aye, take one or two of these," pointing to his family of five girls. She really thought that they might be put in the sack, although her older sisters knew that it was his little joke.

There was also the Windmill man who came from time to time to collect jam jars, which he would exchange for model windmills that he had constructed out of colourful wallpaper. The poorer the traders were, the more onerous their form of transport; the old man who used to sell paraffin and old household utensils had to push his handcart up Elsfield hill to be able to earn a few coppers.

But at least they weren't tramps. And there was always a trail of them, carrying their worldly belongings in a red kerchief tied to a stick that they carried over their shoulder. They would trudge the villages in search of a handout of food and some casual labour. We were always told that if we fed them they would put a mark on the house to inform other tramps that this was a soft option; but we did give them bread and dripping and a cup of milk or hot cocoa all the same. There were some regulars, like the one who came to the Warners every Sunday morning for his sausage and a cup of tea. There were also plenty of poachers from far and wide, as a trapped rabbit would eke out their meagre earnings, and there was also quite a trade in rabbit skins at ½d a pelt.

Gypsies were always a part of our lives; we tolerated them, but we did feel superior to them and called them 'Gippos', but never to their face. Their gaily painted horse-drawn caravans enhanced my romantic idea of their free roaming lives, mostly inspired by the songs we sang at school: 'What care I for my goose feather bed? I'm off with the raggle taggle gypsies, O'. They had the right to pitch camp in Gipsy Corner: a broad roadside triangle of lush grass where the nightingales had also made their abode. Unfortunately this little paradise was adjacent to our most lush meadows and they always managed to come when the standing grass was just ready to be mown. Their horses must have been literally in clover when their masters picked the lock on the chain and let them have their fill of moon daisies, vetch, purple orchids and every variety of wild flower. My father would chase them when he finally got word of what was happening, but by this time more grass had been trampled under hoof than eaten. He would finally get the reluctant horses back into their triangle with much shouting and swearing with threats of the police, which he didn't carry out.

He recalled that on one occasion, a few days later, that a gipsy woman came down the village road selling bunches of white heather. At a certain distance, she was flattering him with praise of his 'kind' face, but when she got near she recognised that face and let out a string of abuse that any docker would have been proud of, "You little scum! You rat face!" And this was the expurgated edition that he selected as he recounted it to us children. Mrs Warner had a similar experience. She always used to give them a slice of bread and dripping, but one day, when a gipsy woman approached her asking her to buy something and she said no, she was told, "You're a pretty woman, but you've got an evil eye." After that her children used to ask, "Which is your evil eye, Mum?" These incidents were not common; we tolerated each other and we relied on them for our clothes pegs, which they made out of willow and sold from door to door throughout the village.

Old Jimmy Stroud was the vet, who would toil up the hill from Oxford with his ramshackle bike in all weathers if there was a horse with colic or a cow with her calf in a difficult breach position. He had bandy legs encased in laced boots and tight gaiters, with a diminutive body and an overlarge head and he looked for all the world like Rumpelstiltskin. I could never keep my eyes off him, particularly his bulbous nose with whiskers emerging from his nostrils in profusion. But my greatest fascination was with his gnome-like ears. The first time I saw him I had to be silenced by a stern look from my mother when I asked in a piercing sotto voice, "But Mam, why has he got whiskers coming out of his ears?"

He remained an enigma, for when my father gave him a cheque, he fumbled in his sagging pockets pulling out a grimy piece of crumpled paper; it was the previous cheque already months old and with a casual, "That'll go with the last one," he pocketed them both. Whether they ever saw the light of day I never knew, but I am sure that my father made it up with cash in the long run as, although we were always short of money, he would never have taken advantage of such a lack of interest in money matters.

There was a time, for many months, when Mr. Stroud stopped coming. I heard whispers about how he had "taken pity on a young girl," which made no sense to me. I had no conception of abortion, nor conception for that matter. Apparently it was quite common for girls 'in trouble' to appeal to the local vet to help them out. I gathered later that his undoing was that, through lack of hygiene, the affair turned septic and the discovery resulted in his prison sentence.

There were no such repercussions from his work with the farm animals. He was a wonder to behold at giving horses a 'drench', thrusting it down their throats with an old cow horn with a hole pierced at the point and he was equally adapt at putting his arm right into the cow's womb to pull out a breached calf, I would always creep round to the loose box to watch him in action and everyone was too concerned about the seriousness of the situation to notice me peeping over the barrier.

The outside world only occasionally intruded on our isolation. One such was Gabriel d'Este, an ageing ballet dancer, who had suffered a nervous break-down and was convalescing as a paying guest with an aunt and uncle of ours who had a farm at Chalton-on-Otmoor. John Collet, the uncle, was a red-faced, pot-bellied horse dealer who would supply the gentry with hacks and hunters and had a "Hail fellow, well met" approach to them, very different from the subservience they mostly enjoyed. So it was through these connections that a dancer from Pavlova's company, who had been on a world tour with her, came to lodge in such primitive surroundings: cold stone floors and damp mildewed rooms. Otmoor had once been a huge inland lake and it still bore the traces by flooding its fields as soon as it rained heavily, as if to recapture its earlier existence.

Gabriel seemed to take to this mixture of rough living and fantasy, just as he took to walking the five miles across the fields to visit us. He charmed my mother with his old-world courtesy, like kissing her hand, lifting it to his lips with an elegant sweep of his arm. It was surely the first time that this had ever happened to her in real life and she responded warmly with tea, cakes and sympathy. His whole presence called out his need for such empathy, with his cadaverous face, dominated by huge imploring eyes, black surrounded by dark rings barely distinguishable from the rest of his perpetual 'five o'clock', which did not have the fashionable trend of today.

His hobby was 'Barbizon' work, which seemed to consist of sticking porcelain fruits onto objects such as china candlesticks. My mother was delighted with her pale green candlestick, lush with bright red strawberries, and she was even more delighted with his apparent fondness for my brother, who had grown into a handsome robust teenager. He greatly admired Monty's strength and earthiness and would accompany him wherever he was working on the farm calling him the pet name of 'Bunny'. We all remarked how fond he had become of Monty, but I am convinced that we were quite innocent of the implications and so indeed was Monty, as I gather that there was no further indication of his feelings.

I wondered why he wasn't fond of me in the same way and one day, when I was cycling to Woodeaton and offered to walk part of the way home to Otmoor with him, he accepted with dignity, but I could tell there was none of the same enthusiasm which made his eyes light up as he walked and talked with my brother. He thanked me politely for my trouble, but I knew that he would never call me by a pet name.

People from Other Villages

The people I knew from other villages – and I didn't know that many – were to my mind a bit strange, if not queer (with no aspersions – queer folk was a common expression).

The one that I knew best was Arthur Woodcock, a farmer in Woodeaton, a sprightly man with an impish face and a crop of black curly hair. On rare occasions, his indomitable mother would invite our family to tea, which meant a long trek down the fields. We women were offered milk or tea with home-made sponge cake, whereas the menfolk were regaled with beer, cheese and biscuits in another room. I would have raised the banner for equality between the sexes had I not preferred sponge cake to the only sip of beer that I had surreptitiously tasted, and I understood why it was called 'bitter'.

I endured sitting quietly while the grown-ups talked, or rather Mrs. Woodcock held sway, because I could not take my eyes off the two cut-glass ornaments, with prisms hanging from them, chiming in the wind. As they moved, they caught the sunlight, creating flashes of all the colours of the rainbow. Today, I am making a miniature fountain with these same prisms dangling round it and the water flowing down them. The other silent member of the women's tea party was Florrie Woodward, the spinster destined to look after her mother. She was so intimidated that, if she ever tried to speak, she put her hand right over her mouth to hide what I imagined was a sort of speech defect, but in retrospect I believe it was a sort of apology for having dared to give voice. In any case, her words were few; her role was to listen to orders, punctuated by a series of reprimands.

When Mrs. Woodcock finally died, Arthur, who felt that he was in his prime, began rather belatedly to sow his wild oats. His first attempt was with a Miss Hay, aptly named as a riding instructress, with whom my father had arranged a few riding lessons for me in exchange for some oats for her horse. I wasn't expecting Arthur Woodcock to join us, but he rode up with Miss Hay, looking very spruce in his new riding kit. All I recall of the lesson is that his horse ran away and my pony followed suit (Darkie, not Dot, by then). It did not take long for both of us to be thrown when our steeds came to a sudden halt. As Miss Hay cantered gracefully to the scene, Arthur's horse and my pony were grazing disdainfully nearby and I felt I detected a similar sentiment reflected in Miss Hay's expression.

That was the end of Arthur's courtship of Miss Hay, as he was soon giving his whole attention to a more sophisticated widow from London. His enthusiasm towards her was boundless; she had insisted on marriage, I gather, and I overheard him saying to my father in sotto voce that she was a 'wonner'. I thought to myself, "Why make a secret of that," being quite unaware of the imputation.

Alas, it was only a month or so later when he came with a very different tale; she had taken over everything: his life, the farm. It had gone to rack and ruin and she was a real tyrant. The little pigs had the run of the house, the chickens would come in and out through the doors or the windows and her dogs had taken over. The timid Florrie had taken refuge with her married sister and he was cornered. I never learnt what happened to them after that.

George Stace, Miss Stace's elder brother, was an infrequent visitor to the village; mostly he came to the school as an informal inspector and I gather that he approved of his sister's achievements. Did Warner recalls how when he came, Miss Stace would say, "Kathie stand up and sing something" and Did would sing a lullaby, "Roses whisper good night." She also remembered how he always wanted to see the drill class, where we all performed in our knickers pulled over our frocks.

He once took me to Oxford in his little three-wheeler Morgan. It was a bright red and we had the hood down so that the wind blew in my face and I felt, "This is the life." We went to a bookshop and he asked me if I would choose a book for a "nice little girl I know." She was apparently about my age and I chose the one I would really like to have had myself. We then went to have tea at Fullers, with slice of two-tier walnut iced cake; I was in my element. Then he took me home and, to my surprise, gave me the book he had intended to give to the nice little girl.

My mother had a very different kind of outing when he took her to the dentist to have all of her teeth out, which was the custom by the time people had reached middle age. She came back with her head enveloped in an enormous shawl to protect her from a biting wind. I wondered, "Perhaps he couldn't ever put the hood up."

He was a great support, especially to his sister; he even took the most recalcitrant Elsfield boys to his school in Headington, where he was headmaster. They came back rather subdued. There were also more joyful occasions when we shared our sport days or had joint country dance sessions.

Mr. Mortimer was the vicar of our neighbouring village, Marston. I don't recall him ever coming to Elsfield, but his reputation for good deeds was well known to us. One story I remember about him was when we were having a laugh at his expense, which was characteristic of Elsfield's view of anyone from another village.

Apparently Mr. Mortimer was walking down Marston road when he saw a horse stretched out apparently dead in the road. His master was sitting beside him, devastated at his unexpected loss, as he was the rag-and-bone man and his livelihood depended on his dilapidated cart being drawn by his equally dilapidated horse. Mr. Mortimer rose to the occasion magnificently and, when he had heard the whole story, he offered to pay for a new steed, which the heartbroken man assured him he could get through a friend for a 'couple of quid'. Mr Mortimer went on his way rejoicing, radiating a truly benign expression. After an appropriate time, the horse was given the signal to rise again and they too departed rejoicing!

I learnt later of his many other good deeds; he was frequently seen getting on the Marston bus to Oxford in his carpet slippers, always with his dog under his arm, and there he would supervise the free meals once a day for tramps in St Clements. He donated one hundred pounds a year for this and kept it up for forty years. He was an old Etonian.

Chapter 7

Pursuits and Activities

We made our own fun and entertainment, both in our play and what the village provided for us. Whenever we could we were roaming the fields and woods, feeling free as the wind. The grown-ups knew that we would be safe and so we never worried. Our favourite games were variations of hide-and-seek, especially Fox and Hounds, as described in games we played on the farm. When we were younger 'Under Elms' was an ideal place for playing houses; there were lots of cubby-holes where no one could see you and we delighted in making mud pies with elderberries for fruit.

What we picked during our ramblings was according to season. In spring there would be sticky buds and catkins, and always pussy willows for Palm Sunday, soon followed by primroses, violets, anemones, cowslips and large oxlips. In summer there was every variety of meadow flower: moon daisies, scabious, corn cockle, bee, butterfly and fly orchids, besides quantities of early purple orchis. It did not matter how many we picked, as there were so many their absence could not be noticed and we all made daisy chains and poppy ladies. The autumn brought food galore: nuts (we looked for sixers and even seveners), blackberries and the most delicious mushrooms, well manured by the carthorses. In winter we could generally find some holly with berries and once, on Christmas Day, we found primroses on a sheltered bank. Whatever the season, we would make sure that we brought home some wood for firing when we wandered over the fields and woods. This was the girls' seasonal gathering.

The boys roamed too, but always for bird's nesting and they collected a whole variety of eggs, blowing them and then placing them according to size in chocolate boxes filled with sawdust. Not to be outdone, I had my own collection and said I was the only person I knew who collected snail shells, and I had some beauties.

I also organised my own club, the Little Feasts Club; it was no coincidence that I was the instigator, as all my life I have been a devotee of feasting. The rules were very simple: we could collect anything from our gardens or from nature, as long as it was edible, and then share the feast together. In really lean times it might be only 'bread and cheese' (young hawthorn shoots) and tiny, new beech shoots. But as summer came, our gardens could be raided for baby carrots, radishes, peas, spinach leaves and especially our own red and yellow raspberries, which grew in what we called 'the jungle'. As for autumn, there was a bonanza: blackberries and hazel nuts in abundance. There were also our Blenheim and conference trees in the deserted cottage, with no risk of Mr. Hill's whip on our legs as, unlike the unfortunate scrumpers, we owned them.

I was completely ignorant about what the boys got up to, other than bird's nesting in the spring. My brother informed me that even that pursuit had its dangers and you had to run if the gamekeeper was about, as you were not supposed to go down fields other than your own. They went for miles around, especially to Otmoor, which was a paradise for waterfowl. Fishing was an attraction and there was always the hope of catching trench or perch with their home-made fishing rods, but this was very rare.

There was no vandalism: just the occasional scrumping, which has been dealt with elsewhere, and a bit of knocking on doors and then running. Most of the boys were kept busy helping with the farm work or the allotment.

Monty did confide in me a glimpse of some of the more dangerous activities they indulged in, "Make bombs of copper tube blocked at one end and two little holes drilled down at the bottom end, and gunpowder down the tube, put a match to it and run like hell!" It must have been successful as he heard that someone had blown the top of his finger off. I don't think they tried after that.

The other unlawful activity was to make magnifying glasses out of discarded hurricane lamps, then concentrate the sun's rays and start a fire. Apparently they also used to play with acetylene lamps, "We used to spit on them to give off a fizz: with water at the top and carbide at the bottom, the water would drip, which lit the acetylene gas. When we ran out of water, we used to pee in it and that was just as good!"

In the summer, picnics were a regular part of our lives, especially for the girls. They varied from a few hastily packed sandwiches of bread and jam, slices of cake and a glass beer bottle of hot tea, encased in wrappings of the

Family picnic in the lane. Monty, in sailor outfit, is second from the right.

Daily Mail, to a much more elaborate affair with a washing up bowl and even sometimes a primus stove. Our favourite place was a clearing in Stow Wood, about half a mile away; it had been an old stone pit, now grown over with tiny pimpernels and harebells and fine grass.

I always had this idea of the magic of picnics and lost no opportunity to initiate one. Once, when my mother was particularly busy, I demanded a picnic and she managed to conjure up some cake and a bottle of powdered lemonade, Eiffel Tower. I had to go on my own and only got as far as the other side of the five barred gate to the Little Field adjoining the farm. My dogged munching was rudely interrupted by a series of missiles landing all around me. They were cowpats, fortunately dry ones, which my brother was aiming from the other side of the hedge!

The village was vibrant with activities to suit everyone; for us children there was the Girl's Friendly Society, held at the vicarage with Miss Stace in attendance, where we were encouraged in our creativity: painting, modelling and papier maché. The boys linked up with the men when they were a bit older and tried their hand at billiards in the reading room attached to the school. Mothers, with their babies, were encouraged to come to the vicarage once a week to the Mother's Union. All the women joined the Women's Institute meetings held in the Manor once a month and the great offshoot of that firmly established organisation was the Drama club. Together with the

The little field where I had my picnic.

concerts, pageants, dances and whist drives there was a hive of activity and entertainment.

In summer, there was cricket, played every Saturday in the Home Close field bordering on Under Elms. We always went to watch, armed with bottles of cherry cider and an assortment of sherbet dabs, liquorice allsorts and toffees. We didn't follow the intricacies of the game; it was just fun to see the young men, resplendent in white trousers and shirts, running, bowling and especially getting bowled out. Later, at the secondary school, I was elected into the team for what should have been a glorious occasion. I had inadvertently developed a sort of googly in bowling, which devastated the batsmen and wickets went flying in all directions. To my horror, when it came to the actual match, I had a dose of nerves and, far from pitching my half volleys down the pitch, all I achieved was a ball that went almost vertically up into the air! The crowning shame was when I had to continue for the rest of the over, with a repeat of the high soaring ball. There was relief all around when the six balls had been sent upwards and I could be taken off for good.

In the winter the village events were mostly in the evenings and, as there was no notion of having a baby-sitter, I always accompanied the family to anything that was going on: dances, whist drives, concerts. We would walk the length of the village in the dark, with my father lighting the way with a big hurricane lamp. It was quite eerie, with the shadows of the elm trees towering above us and sometimes the moon, clear as a bell, seeming to follow us as it darted in and out of the clouds.

Village Concerts

I only have vague memories of the village concerts, which were superseded by the whist drives and dances; this was a pity as they were not only very popular but also great levellers in that the people from the Manor joined in with the farmers and all the workers. Prices were reasonable, ranging from 6d to a shilling with the cheapest seats at the back and the children admitted free, sitting on the floor right under the artistes' noses. Thick curtains over the door kept out the cold and also anyone who might try to sneak in, but this was rare as everyone had a job or a trade.

First on the scene was Mrs. Buchan, who would give a heart rendering version of, "You must rise and call me early mother, for I'm to be queen of the May mother, for I'm to be queen of the May." I can recall the rapture on her face as she made the tears flow. Her daughter Alice's speciality was the song, "For I would be a dancer, a dancer all in yellow-o, Said the frog to the fish again-eo." The Buchans spoke with an aristocratic accent, far removed from the broad Oxfordshire that most of us were brought up to speak. So when Jack Nappin, the blacksmith, got up to sing with gusto, "Give I lots of pudding, Give I any kind of duff, plum or spotted, that's the stuff; I don't care what sort it is, as long as it's a good 'un'," there was quite a contrast. Jack lived on his own, but next door to his sister, who no doubt supplied him with pudding.

Then there was Mr. Paintin, a farm labourer, who always created a loving relationship with his 'Little Brown Jug', with such a knowing twinkle in his eye, expressing perhaps fond memories of the Saturday night walk to the pub at Marston. But who was it who always recited the 'Green eye of the little yellow God'? It always sent shivers down my back at the tender age of five or six.

Finally there was the trio, who later played for the dances. There was my mother at the piano, the vicar full of animation with his fiddle and Amos Wing from Beckley on the 'cello. They would play a mixture of dance tunes and folk songs, which everyone joined in, or they would also provide a peaceful accompaniment to the gentile strains of the Watts girls' duets.

Friday Nights

One of the highlights, to while away the long winter evenings, was the Friday lantern lectures and sing songs. We were fascinated by this early precursor of the electronic age: the Magic Lantern. The organisation was probably in the hands of our 'betters' and the lecture subjects seemed to be chosen more for the experiences of the visiting lecturers than for our own rather restricted orientation. I can only recall one, where the speaker had been on a climbing holiday in Serbia; most of the slides were of her in full climbing gear, knickerbockers and all. It was somewhat repetitive, but we children soon cottoned on to the way in which the slides were changed: the speaker tapping the floor with her demonstrating stick. So, when we were bored, which was often the case, there were several taps, which threw the speaker into confusion as the slides went flashing past and the lecture was hastened towards its end, when there were refreshments, including little iced cakes, which were possibly our main incentive to come.

The audience for the lectures was mostly composed of women and their daughters. As one of the boys put it, "Tain't very often that we went," but they turned up for the sing songs which were much more animated and it was Captain Kettlewell who held us in his thrall. He was an old naval man. He would get us singing shanty songs and we reflected his vigorous enthusiasm with equal vigour. His long white beard swayed in rhythm to the notes banged out on the piano by his wife with appropriate zeal. Favourites were 'Shenandoah', 'What shall we do with a drunken sailor' and 'Johnny come down to Hilo'. Some years later my mother was given a book of sea shanties for her work as treasurer of the Women's Institute and we re-echoed the same animation round the piano on a Sunday night.

Dances and Whist Drives

The school was the venue for all of the many village events. The partition between the infants' and the big room was taken down and the 'reading' room left for the men who didn't want to participate and preferred billiards. On special occasions, it became the refreshment room with the billiards table duly covered with a white tablecloth.

The dances were very lively affairs with my mother in her stride at the piano, strumming out: 'Yes sir, that's my baby' and 'Yes, we have no bananas'. Both puzzling, for surely anyone would know whose baby it was and did they mean yes or no on the question of bananas? The vicar, who accompanied her on his fiddle, was in fine form after a little refreshment. His ample face would glow a deep red, as his body swayed to the pulse of the beat, and his rather corpulent outline would take on an almost mystical trance. It was not so far removed from his towering figure in the pulpit, both filling me with a certain fascination and awe. The third member of the trio was Amos Wing from Beckley; true to his name he was an Ariel type figure and played with such gusto that he reminded me of a magic lantern figure drawn through at speed.

I had ample time to observe this detail, as I had to be brought along when my father and brother came to the men's club in the reading room. I did feel left out always when the women sat round the room and the young men would make their choice of whom to dance with, for all the world like a farmer inspecting which cow to buy. They never chose me: eight-year-olds held no appeal for them. I had one glorious moment however, at the Christmas party, when we played Winking. I was so adept at wriggling free from the partner behind, who tried to hold me, that I enjoyed quite a number of kisses with the fellow who had winked at me, even if they were more like pecks on the cheek!

There was always full attendance at the dances and the young ones would never miss them. They only cost 6d and it was an occasion to dress up. Hilda Warner managed to get a quite glamorous dress from the rummage sale, but it was much too long so her mother tacked it up hastily before the dance. When she was dancing with Richard Morby, who was no lightweight, his foot caught in the hem and it all came down, floating round her feet! She was mortified.

The whist drives were a whirl of changing places and partners, with an interval for sandwiches and pink and white iced cakes, which was my chief interest. I did not feel so out of it when I could participate as an equal at the whist drives because of my early training at home; at least I could hold my own and once won the second prize, which was a large sweet jar decorated with rings of blue, green and purple. It was empty.

Drama

Drama was always an integral part of our village life and like the concerts it seemed to cut across class barriers. The initiative came from Mrs. Buchan and later Alice, her daughter, and rehearsals were always held in the august surroundings of the Manor. Oxfordshire was renowned for its drama festivals, with local heats culminating with the finalists competing at Summertown in North Oxford. Elsfield was more than once a winner, having passed the preliminaries at Islip. After one final production, I recall seeing my mother so excited that she could hardly get her words out. "Maud," the judge had said, "Maud, you were excellent!" This was her triumph as 'Maud' in a play called, 'Trifles', the portrayal of a lone woman who cherished her canary, rather like Flaubert's parrot. The judge in question was none other than the famous Tyrone Guthrie and I recall him as a tall distinguished looking man with a neatly trimmed moustache and pointed beard.

In another finalist play, Mrs. Buchan enjoyed a reversal of roles when she played a country yokel, with a battered hat and a straw in his mouth. She entered into the part wholeheartedly and with much aplomb, however Tyrone Guthrie did spot an incongruous gold bracelet showing from under her (or his) rough smock with the electric light reflecting on it. I didn't see the Emperor's New Clothes, which she produced at Kirtlington, but it was renowned by the fact that a little girl in the audience jumped the gun and called out, "But he hasn't got any clothes on!"

Another triumph was 'The room at the Inn', where Mrs. Hambidge, who kept the village shop and post office, scored a great success as the flamboyant sergeant. Much later I persuaded my classmates to choose it for the school play. Sensing that it was veering towards being a flop, I had the nerve to go to the Manor and ask to borrow the blunderbuss – I somehow thought that it would lift the production. It was not surprising that I was confronted by the austere Scottish butler; the very one who had managed to convey his disapproval when I had come late for the distribution of Easter eggs. This time he displayed the same sentiments as he delivered the message, "As the weapon is very old, it cannot be borrowed." I realise now what a cheek it was to ask.

Meanwhile there were less ambitious attempts at drama in the village. Miss Stace, whose influence far exceeded her role as headmistress, staged rehearsals for small plays. Her patience was sometimes tried to the utmost, as when an aspirant actor could not bring himself to pronounce 'outhouse' without emphasising the 'th': as he insisted, "There it was in print." Another one would insist on saying the word, "Ahem" instead of coughing after saying, "Good morning" in a meaningful way as a detective. No matter how many times he tried, he always ended up in saying the word "Ahem!" Such was the power of the written word. Once, in a murder play, a dagger was used with the blade going up the handle; this caused consternation as many of the younger children thought the victim had been really stabbed.

The tradition of drama was carried on by the Buchan boys, Billie and Alistair. They turned an old building into 'The Barn Theatre'. There was a very big stage adapted somehow from a chicken house and a laundry. They got Betty Webb, who was artistic, to paint two masks on the door: tragedy and comedy; but that was the only participation from the rest of us, they were probably improvising rather than giving performances.

But there was another type of drama that brought us out of the village to Oxford and Blenheim: these were the pageants. My memories of them were somewhat hazy, as they must have occurred when I was quite young. Apparently there was a grand one at Worcester College, with the backdrop of the lake and where I was only a spectator. I remember Bessie Phipps dressed up as a chocolate girl selling cigarettes with thin black stockings and very high heels; she was in her element, far from her struggles over arithmetic or more likely doing the washing up. Looking back she was really sexy, but that notion didn't occur to me at the time. Apparently all the actors went for drinks in one of the students' rooms and it was one of the very hottest days of that summer. It was the same evening in fact when one of the gardeners at the Manor dropped dead of sunstroke. He had been carrying water in his horse-drawn cart all day to the vegetable garden and then to the allotments and there was some veiled talk of a connection between the two events, his death and the pageant. There was a feeling of "as soon as our back is turned, something

happens in the village," like when Mr. Watts's five cows were struck by lighting the day when most of the villagers were at the Wembley exhibition for their annual outing.

The occasion that I remember well was when the whole village took part in a medieval pageant at Blenheim and this time there were no repercussions in the village left behind. I think it was to mark

A water carrier.

some royal anniversary and Princess Margaret was in attendance. Bessie Phipps was again enjoying herself, this time as Alice Buchan's page. My mother was a lady if not a queen and she certainly behaved herself as if she was royalty. She was swathed in a long powder blue robe with a girdle and a high pointed wimple, with more powder blue round her neck and then trailing and flowing into an extensive train, which I found great difficulty in controlling. I was her page with a green tunic and long green stockings and a Robin Hood hat with a feather in it.

The pageant must have been of a market day as we were all milling around buying things; I thought at the time, why does such a lady have to go shopping in the market? Things came to a head when my mother started buying five huge sacks of wool, "What on earth did we want those for?" "How much would they cost?" She intimated that this was no way for a page to behave to his courtly mistress, so I resumed my role, completely mystified by her eccentric behaviour.

The pageants were good fun, even if I didn't always get the hang of grown-ups playing like we children did; but they seem to vanish like the village concerts, and the amateur drama. We only once went to the cinema as a village outing and that was to see Robert Donat in the Thirty Nine Steps, written by John Buchan. Much later on it was the custom to go to the Electric cinema every Saturday on the two o'clock bus and afterwards to the milk bar, which had just come into fashion, but that was a different kind of life.

It took me a long time before I would venture into a cinema, as I was taken at the tender age of three when we went to Liverpool for a holiday. I can still see the huge faces bearing down on me from the screen and I yelled my head off until my reluctant mother took me out. It was certainly her first opportunity to see a film. I don't think she ever went again until I was in my late teens; was it the occasion when I had gone surreptitiously with the village blacksmith and found, to our mutual consternation, that she was sitting just behind us? I should add that it was a different blacksmith; this young one was from the village we had moved to.

Fox Hunting

The whole village was alerted when the South Oxfordshire Hunt descended upon us like a pack of cards with much bugle blowing and barking of the hounds. They might have descended from outer space for all we knew, but we did know that they were sure to come.

When they met at our farm, they accepted our tots of sherry, which we could ill afford, as of their right (de seigneur?) with barely an acknowledgement. My mother, who stood in admiring awe of the gentry, was known to protest that they didn't even say thank you.

I put our relationship to the ultimate test on the only occasion when I dared to follow the hunt on 'Old Dot', my shaggy pony, who was probably the equivalent of a human eighty years old. Dot usually had to be urged, coaxed and slapped into a trot, let alone a canter, except for her favourite last lap gallop home; but the hunting sounds brought forth memories of her youth and pricking up her ears and neighing ecstatically, she plunged into the chase at full gallop. I was in no position to restrain her, let alone reconsider the wisdom of joining in. All my energies were concentrated on holding tight.

It was a 'John Gilpin' situation, where we were in the forefront instead of a lowly position well in the rear, as befitted our station. The outraged anger of the huntsmen cut me just as if they had used their crops, which they wisely reframed from attempting, as they realised that whipping Dot from the back could incite her to consolidate her advanced position or even lead the field. I was saved this dubious honour when everyone had to slow down to pass through a narrow open gateway, the hedges being too high to jump, even for the most intrepid rider. My troubles were not over when halfway through Dot displayed a bad attack of claustrophobia: she started backing with as much ferocity as she had shown in going forward. I had as much control of the situation as I had had during the big gallop and I was showered with abuse from all sides. "Get that damn pony out of the way!" Nothing was nearer to my desires and fortunately I was given a clear passage backwards, as, rather than risk having their precious thoroughbreds kicked, they had all made way themselves. (I thought afterwards it was like the crossing of the Red Sea, only in reverse).

And there we were – finally at a standstill, the spirit taken out of us. Dot was recovering from the unaccustomed exercise, standing stock-still and panting with her whole body so that I felt as if I was on a jerky rocking horse. My feelings were a mixture of shame and ignominy, but I was relieved to be once more in control of a docile, but unrepentant Dot, as had always been the case until now.

During our mad chase at the forefront, I had been possessed of a deep-down fear: that of being 'blooded', having once seen a fox torn to pieces and a young girl smeared with its blood. This had added to my panic, when we seemed to be winning what Dot obviously thought was a Grand National type of race. The practice of 'blooding' was to smear the fox's blood all over the face and hands of the one, usually a child, whose first kill it was and they were also given the prized brush. I needn't have worried; these rituals were reserved for the 'set' and would not have been extended to an outsider like myself.

After that episode, I joined the village children as we ran panting after the chase. Sometimes we were in a better position to spot the fox when it cut back frantically to try to mislead its relentless pursuers. Then we would clap cup our hands and make a far-reaching, "Alloo – alloo – alloo," whereupon the chase, both huntsmen and hounds, would veer round in our direction as if by magic. The exact technique must have been inherited by the village children, because when my mother attempted the same thing when she saw the fox right in the farmyard, she was shouted at by the master, "Shut your damned mouth, woman!" She never felt quite the same about these huntsmen who rode roughshod over our fields and on feelings.

We children could never miss a hunt and, when we finally arrived still breathless for school, most of the morning had gone and sometimes most of the afternoon too. In the old days, the punishment was automatically caning and it was accepted as the price that had to be paid. But since Dolly Lafford broke the cane over her knee, caning was limited to the boys, whereas we were given words to learn. Miss Stace knew that she could never stop us from following the hounds. She would say in a very cross voice when we came rushing in, puffing away to pretend that we had been running hard to get back to school, "Where have you been?" "Hunting, Miss." Once Did Warner had fallen and hurt her knee badly and Miss Stace's comment was, "Serves you right."

Not one of us children gave much thought to the fox, let alone having pity for it; we had been brought up to believe that this was all in the nature of things. Besides they said if you tried to shoot a fox, you probably would only wound it and it would die a slow lingering death of poisoning. In any case it was sheer heresy to talk of shooting a fox and tenant farmers knew that it would be more than their livelihood was worth. So the justification continued; smoking them out of their dens was considered cruel, especially

if they had cubs and I only learnt later that the foxes were being specially bred to keep up the numbers to hunt. We actually believed the grown-ups when they assured us that in this way the fox had a sporting chance and some went so far as to assert that the fox quite enjoyed the chase!

From our point of view, farming people depended a lot on their chickens, which were everlastingly being killed by the fox. I remember vividly one moonlight night when my father got up from his sickbed – he had 'flu at the time – and chased the fox right over the fields in his nightshirt. I believe that in the end the fox dropped the squawking hen in his need to outrun his pursuer and, in any case, my father was no match for foxes when it came to speed. But he returned in triumph, to the admonitions of my mother who then had to nurse him through an attack of bronchitis.

I was watching this drama from my window in my nightdress; this vision of the fleeting shadow of the fox carrying a large white Wyandotte hen and my father in hot pursuit. The thought struck me that it was just like a comic cartoon. We always shut up the hen houses at night; this was one of my jobs and the hen must have decided to have a night out in the nearby fields, which almost cost her life.

The cackling protests from all the hen houses showed that they knew only too well what was happening. They had good reason to be afraid as, when vixens have cubs to suckle, they can be driven to steal the fowl in broad daylight and, as all of our chickens took full advantage of being free range, they were always vulnerable.

When I went to the secondary school at Oxford that was the end of my hunting experiences and my sentiments consolidated in favour of the fox. My family continued discreetly to show little enthusiasm for the hunt and all that remained in our house was a hunting horn left by the huntsmen as a souvenir and, although the whole family blew on it until their eardrums ached, they could not produce more than a forlorn whine between them.

Chapter 8

Festivals and Celebrations

The biggest festival of the year was of course Christmas, followed by Easter, but there were also regular highlights such as May Day and, the most important one for me, my birthday on August 15th. Summer was a time for the annual outing, village fêtes and what we called 'bun-fights' at the vicarage. Then the autumn heralded the St. Giles fair and bonfire night. We would have felt deprived if the village had missed out on any of these celebrations.

Christmas

This was a time when the lord of the Manor distributed largesse to the farm workers and their families. In old Mr. Parson's day, the gifts were quite specific. Men, women and children all had to go to the Manor to receive their presents. The women received dress pieces, a length of calico or flannel and they were allowed to give their choice. The married men received shirting, sufficient to make two shirts (another job for the women). Householders all had a leg, loin or shoulder of mutton, depending on the size of the family, and single men had a breast of lamb and presumably no shirting.

The school children were asked in at the front door, where tables of Christmas cards were placed, and they could each choose one together with an orange. Then came the giving of the children's clothes. The boys had a suit and the parents were given two shillings and sixpence to buy a cap. The girls were given cloth for a red and black check dress one year and the following year material for a black coat. The clothes were made up by Mrs. Allam's mother and, when she died, Mrs. Allam took on the sewing. The girls also had a cotton frock in pink and white check for the summer and a straw hat with a band and bow of red ribbon. It seems that the boys just had a red tie at that time, presumably because they could make do with knickerbockers all the year round and the tie would go with their shirt. For several years, the girls were in luck as a white linen coat was bestowed annually, but then it was deemed unnecessary, so Miss Parsons cancelled it.

The Christmas party was always held in the dining room of the Manor House, with a large Christmas tree in the centre and all around the room were trestle tables with a present for each child and also one from a draw. The tea was held in the Servants' hall with two large Christmas cakes, one for boys and one for girls, and after the feast they all had slices wrapped up for their parents, together with an orange and a tiny ornament off the top of the cake, usually a miniature dog, cat, fox, pig, etc.

I learnt all of this information from Mrs. Allam's account of it; my own memories are when the Buchan's were at the Manor and Miss Parsons had moved to Home Farm. There were still presents from the Manor, but with a difference. There was always a pair of sheets for the farm workers' families; these were made of unbleached calico and, although they looked brown, in the end they bleached in the sun and became softer as time went by. The Buchan boys used to get out the pony and trap and distribute Mrs. Charlock's puddings labelled, "Happy Christmas and please return the basin." There was also a half-pound of tea per family, which was still quite expensive in those days.

For me, the highlight of Christmas was the village party, now at the school, but given by the Buchans. To my mind, the presents at this party were lavish and I still recall how I held up the distribution procedure for what seemed like an eternity, when I was offered the choice of a present. It was between a beautiful book called, 'Dulcie and Tottie' and some notepaper and envelopes. As I dithered, the rapturous bonhomie of the organisers gave way to ill-concealed impatience and still I couldn't make up my mind. My mother was whispering, "Have the book," yet I was sorely tempted by the idea of notepaper all to myself. I finally took my mother's promptings and, when reading it over and over again, as we had few books, I was given an insight into how rich people like the Buchans lived. Dulcie and Tottie had a French governess, whom Tottie did not like, "She calls my dog a she-hang; if he's a hang at all he's a He-hang." All of this and much else went right over my head, but I loved getting the feel of that life. Bessie Phipps wasn't so lucky. Mrs. Buchan gave her a little sewing purse, like an envelope, "Here you are, Bessie, now you'll be able to mend your stockings, because every time I see you you've got a hole in them." That spoilt the party completely for Bessie, as it would have done for me, especially as it was said in front of the whole village. Agnes Warner was no less satisfied; she complained that she always got a boy's storybook. Looking back, I realise that I was privileged to be given a choice, although they probably regretted their act of class distinction when I held up the procedure.

Miss Parson's Christmas tea was less formal; there were trays of Christmas cards on the trestles and we jostled and snatched in a sort of frenzied free-for-all, with none of the order and discipline of the previous régime. Miss Parson stood watching us, smiling benevolently as always, as we made our way to the long table for tea, clutching our cards like trophies of war. We children never seemed to appreciate this bounty, taking it as our due, even with muttered criticisms. Fortunately, Miss Parsons had no inkling of our feelings. She probably thought we were full of happy gratitude as she stood there. We calmed down as we munched our way through dainty sandwiches and little iced cakes until there was nothing left, rather like a swarm of locusts. The finale was when Edith, the buxom cook, would roll oranges down the long trestle table until every child had one to take home.

Decorating the church was a great co-operative effort; first the women and the big girls and boys helped to collect the evergreens and bring them to the church, together with the irons and lathes on which the wreaths were made. Smaller fry, like my friends and me, collected holly and ivy for Christmas and then, at Easter, we excelled ourselves picking primroses, violets, bluebells and anemones to decorate the church windows. Then the work began: fixing everything with string to keep them from sliding down from the windowsills. The boys vied with each other to fetch the balls of string from the gardener, Mr. Gould. But they kept running short of string and he accused the boys of putting great wads of it in their pockets, so after that the boys were not allowed to 'help'. Finally on the Saturdays before the church festivals, the gardeners, with the ladies of the Manor and vicarage, came to put the finishing touches to the decorations with flowers and they certainly made a blaze of colour against the green.

The only other village activity that I just remember were the mummers, who came, I'm told, from Holton. One was dressed up as a bear, which I took

Maypole dance in an Oxfordshire village, 1916. © Oxfordshire County Council Photographic Archive.

for real and was ultra cautious of approaching too near. There was also a sketch of a dentist pulling a huge tooth out – again a bit scary for me. After that we heard no more of the mummers.

May Day was the next big event that the village celebrated and, in the old days, the teacher, Mrs. Allam, would make a May Day garland. Her rather mystifying account of how it was constructed was as follows, "This consisted of three thick sticks tied together and placed over the top, three hoops of different sizes and then two more sticks for the girls to carry." At the school, they chose the May Queen and also a May King and, all dressed in white, they visited every house in the village singing our May Day song, "'Tis the first of May, we're happy and gay and at your door I stand, Turn your head not away, but with us be gay, because it's new May morning. A brush of May I have brought you and I can no longer stay. So God bless you all both great and small and I wish you a Merry, Merry May." Mrs. Allam continued, "Then we were called, all marched up in twos from the school by our governess to the Manor House and the garland was slung up from the ceiling over the table that was spread with a delicious tea. Then we had games in the field at the bottom of the Manor with two swings in the trees, one for the boys and one for the girls. Each child was given a share in the takings which amounted to about 9d each."

I heard about these great May Day celebrations, but by the time I was old

enough, it had taken the form of the more conven-
tional Maypole dance at the school for the
villagers to watch. There was a gaily
painted pole and silk ribbons
attached to the top, all of different
colours. The idea was that each child
had a ribbon and danced one, two,
three, hop round the maypole twirling in
and out until it was just one long stick and
then unravelling until every ribbon was
stretched out like a multi-coloured medieval tent.

There was only one child in the whole school
who could not master the intricate one,
two, three, hop and, to my lasting
shame, I was not allowed to
take part in the display. I
realise that now just one
'rogue' dancer would ruin the
whole effect and there would have
been chaos. It wasn't the 'under and
over' that flummoxed me, it was when
you did the hop. I could have managed an elegant run, but alas it was 'one,
two, three, hop'; so I huddled as far as possible out of sight of the rows of
admiring parents and tried to look as though I wasn't there.

Easter Celebrations

The village celebrated Easter along the same lines as Christmas, but on a
lesser scale. There was the same lavish decoration of the church with spring
flowers, the same distribution of cards by Miss Parsons, which was somewhat
more dignified, probably because the boys were conspicuous by their absence:
the cards were all of spring flowers which did not appeal to them. They did
turn up in the afternoon however for the tea of hot cross buns and cakes and
of course the ceremony of the rolling of oranges.

The Manor was not to be outdone however and I realise that there was
some unspoken rivalry between the old and the new régimes. On Good Friday
afternoon at two o'clock, we would gather at the Manor House for a distribution of a hot cross bun, an Easter egg and an orange each. One Easter I was
late and, to my dismay, the massive oak door was shut by the time I arrived
and the whole assembly of the village children were munching away with
pitying looks at my misfortune. I plucked up my courage and banged on the

The front door of the manor, where the Parsons and later the Buchans lived.

door, "Please I haven't had my hot cross-bun, nor my Easter egg, nor my orange." The butler eyed me disdainfully and retreated without a word, returning with my three spoils, which had never tasted so delicious.

But Easter Sunday was always a family affair, with the hiding of chocolate eggs in the garden. There were lots to find as we had also decorated hard-boiled ones with various colours: coffee, cochineal and green colouring, then painted them with exotic patterns. It was the day when we sacrificed one of our precious chickens for Sunday dinner: the one time in the whole year! It was worth waiting for. Then for tea we had made a simnel cake, as had most of the families. We had had difficulty in getting the marzipan balls to stick on round the cake; I was happy to dispense with the obvious solution of putting a layer of greaseproof paper round it, because then I could claim as 'treasure trove' any balls that fell on kitchen floor.

My Birthday Party

I certainly never missed out on my birthday party and most of the village children of my age would expect to come. There was a new family in the village called 'Grimes', and their name did not belie them. In a spirit of condescending philanthropy, I asked my mother if I could invite the Grimes children, but she refused and I was somewhat relieved.

We played in the wagons, round the haystacks and chased the chickens, with the Rhode Island Red cockerels less belligerent in the face of sheer numbers. The highlight for the guests was having rides on Dot, which they called my Shetland pony, but I don't believe Dot had any such credentials. Her behaviour has been described elsewhere, but somehow her sense of rebellion was not apparent on my birthday and she gently ambled round with the

Friends at my birthday party. Left to right, front row: Bessie Phipps, Agnes Warner, me, Did Warner; then Freddie Watts and Betty Webb.

novices on her back, only stopping suddenly now and again to graze some choice grass, with the result that the inexperienced rider would slide gently over her head.

The birthday tea was a triumph: bread and jam sandwiches, iced biscuits with pictures on them and, the crowning glory, the ribbon cake, with three layers of chocolate, pink and yellow. At one party, Freddie Watts placed a large red handkerchief on the snow-white linen table-cloth. The grown-ups made various attempts to persuade him to remove it, but all in vain; at an attempt at persuasion or removal, his reply was uncompromising, "Let it abide. I tell 'ee." So we did.

The Annual Outing

Each year there was the annual outing and almost everybody went, except my father; he was too busy in the summer and, although it was only for the day, it was our one holiday for the year. Mr Dring's char-a-banc was always hired and this was a most exciting vehicle. It seemed to me to be of immense length with rows and rows of long benches, with a door to each row so that we entered on one side only and then shoved along to make room. That was the origin of its name: a sort of chariot with long benches.

Its crowning glory was the enormous hood, which had to be hoisted and rolled over our heads if there was a sudden downpour, but my memory is that almost always we basked in the sun on the way down. On the way back, it was waiting for us already fixed with side panelling to keep us warm in the dark. Mr. Dring seemed to enjoy the trip as much as any of us and we certainly would not have anyone else to take us. There were always two stops on the way back at a pub for the men-folk and we all joined in the raucous singing on the way home, no doubt well lubricated with halves of bitter. The women-folk also indulged in a 'tipple' of stout, but they stayed outside the pub for their men-folk to bring it to them.

The first outing that I recall was to the great exhibition at Wembley and I was too young to appreciate it; it was all confusion to me and endless walking around. Bessie Phipps was gawping about and bumped straight into a lamppost, but then we weren't used to lampposts in Elsfield. The only part of the trip that I liked was the fair with galloping horses and swing boats. What I do remember was that when we arrived home there had been a terrible thunderstorm and five of Mr. Watts's cows had been struck dead under a thunderstorm on Hill field. We went to see them the next day before they were carted to the knacker's yard and the outline of these corpses against the sky is still imprinted on my mind. There was almost a feeling that we shouldn't have gone, as this was the sort of thing that could happen when we deserted the village.

The next outing to Southsea was a complete contrast: for me it was sheer magic; it was the first time I had seen the sea and I have been intrinsically attached to it ever since. We were a bit disappointed that it wasn't sand, expecting every seaside to have quantities of sand as in Alice in Wonderland. It was certainly more difficult to balance when we paddled and, even in the shallow water, Betty Webb was overturned by the waves and had to be rescued by her sister, Win. She said she had thought she was drowned and to her

dismay her silk dress with pink stripes and her white panama hat were all drenched. The rest of us kept more or less dry by tucking our dresses in our knicker elastic. The boys were more venturesome and wandered out to sea as far as they dared, the young ones in short knickerbockers and the big ones with their long trousers rolled up well above their knees. They had their photograph taken in a row, revealing black knees contrasting with pure white

Outing to Southsea. Monty is second from left, Jimmy Maltby fourth, with Perp Newell at the end.

Outing to Cheddar Caves. I am third from the left, hidden under a cloche hat. Mr Dring, the charabanc driver, is on the right. Miss Stace's bull-nosed Morris is in the middle.

legs. The girls missed out on the photograph, but we didn't mind, we were enjoying the splash of the waves against our thighs.

Another memorable visit was to Cheddar Caves and there is a photograph of us all in gathered round Miss Stace's bull-nosed Morris. We were all in our Sunday best, which accounts for the fact that only the bottom half of the girls' faces was visible, as 'cloche' hats were the order of the day. That is with the exception of Bessie Phipps, who had abandoned hers. She had been assigned to the 'dicky' of Miss Stace's car and she said that throughout the long, windswept journey she had been hanging on for dear life.

We had all been issued a notebook and started writing valiantly in spite of the bumpy char-a-banc, but most of us only got as far as what we had for breakfast when we abandoned it to gaze at the ever-changing landscape. We arrived at Wells Cathedral at midday, just in time to see the mechanical figures perform their stately ritual, much to our amazement.

Outing to Bournemouth.

The caves were quite eerie! It was the first time we had seen, or for that matter, heard of stalagmites and stalagmites, let alone wander amongst them. The idea of endless drops of water forming these stalwart 'icicles' intrigued me and to be amongst them in the mysterious darkness sent a shiver down my spine. I decided to remember which was which and hit upon the mnemonic that 'm' came before 't' in the alphabet and therefore was from the ground and the 't's were from the roof and I've just checked and it is still the case!

As ever the highlight of the day for me was the food. One of my besetting sins has been gluttony and this time it reached a peak of gratification. The contrast between the mystique of the caves and material sustenance was overwhelming and the sight of those long tables spread with gleaming white cloths and bowl after bowl of luscious strawberries, alternating with ones full of yellow Somerset cream, was a feast for our hungry eyes. Our elaborate packed lunches, with favourite cheese wafer straws, had gone down in memory long past and here we could have as much as we could eat, which was indeed a tall order. We never had strawberries at home, only raspberries, which were all overgrown in what we called the 'jungle' of both red and yellow fruit and we had to trample out paths when we picked them with large china jugs tied to our waists. Because they were so prolific, I felt that they were rather commonplace compared with these luscious strawberries. How we managed to climb up the 365 steps of Jacob's Ladder after such fare was quite a feat, but I bounded up with the energy of a young deer. Coming down at speed, I was gratified to see my mother watching me with pride, at least that is what I hoped.

Visits to Oxford

Except for walks down the fields on Sunday evenings, we never had family outings: my parents were too busy. I did go shopping to Oxford with my mother, which was a mixed blessing. There was the dread of being in Mr. Willis's carrier's cart; he had never forgotten the butter incident; but there was the exciting lunch at the Cadena Cafe. To my mind this was the height of luxury: palm trees, orchestra, wicker chairs and certainly the best fried plaice with chips and anchovy sauce, followed by strawberry ice cream, that I had ever tasted.

It compensated for the long waits when my mother met some friends, or more likely, relatives. Her brother, Uncle Harold, and his corpulent wife, Aunty Mabel, could always be relied upon to give me suffocating bear hugs, accompanied by rather wet kisses. They had a stall in the covered market to sell their produce in market gardening. I soon learnt that if I continually nudged my mother to finish her endless talk, she would betray me and point out that I was prodding her to go. The adults would all take a poor view of my conduct.

I hated going to Strangers, the hairdressers, as whoever cut my bob and fringe accompanied the snipping with expressions of horror as to how thick it was. Certainly there was an awful lot to sweep up. I am enjoying the bonus now, with no thought of baldness or even thinning hair. Long afterwards, when I was a student, I was treated to a session at Elizabeth Arden's and experienced the same cries of horror at the thickness of my eyebrows, which had never once been tended.

In spite of these contretemps, I loved going to Oxford and took a delight in the college gardens and the Ashmolean and Pitt Rivers museums and, best of all, the Botanical Gardens. One day I wanted to be a student there.

The Annual Village Fête

The village fête was eagerly awaited every year; that was the one time that all the family went. It was usually held in the extensive Manor gardens, with tea in the house if it was wet. The stalls were always brimming with the women's creativity: lavender bags, the bran tub, lace work and cakes of all descriptions. The men all crowded to guess the weight of the pig, donated by the lord of the Manor; the prize was the pig, for the one who guessed the nearest, alternately it was bowling for the pig. Later the men were to flex their muscles in the tug-of-war; while the boys were into 'Torpedoing the Whale', with darts flying all over the big tank and much splashing of water.

The fête that is crystallised in my memory was when it was held in Watts's field, instead of the gentile lawns of the Manor. I was dressed in my Sunday best, which was new for the occasion: yellow straw hat with rosebuds attached and snow white embroidered dress, white socks and patent leather shoes. My father had taken me and I was overcome with all of the attractions, so much so that through sheer exuberance I did a roly-poly down a hilly slope. Unfortunately I was not of an age to be able to distinguish between the Manor gardens and Mr. Watts's pasture-land. The cows had been there the night before, and when I landed at the bottom of the slope, I found to my horror that there were round imprints of a particularly soft cow pat all around my new frock!

Deprived of all dignity, I ran screaming to my father, who took the whole incident in his stride. He plucked a whole handful of grass and proceeded to wipe it all off, while giving me words of comfort; he made me feel that everything was alright and so I enjoyed the rest of the fête. Later, the dress took on a delicate shade of pale blue when the grass stains had been removed with a large dose of the bluebag.

My other memory of a fête was when I was much older. This was in the auspices of the Manor and there was a horseracing stall, which I proved to be a dab hand at. You held a string attached to your horse and by sleight of hand you could jerk it forward to compete with the other three participants. After receiving two prizes of my choice, I was aware that my continual success had transformed the benevolence of the helper to downright hostility, as she saw her store of prizes rapidly being depleted. I moved on.

After the tea and iced cakes, John Buchan organised a competition, which consisted of him holding up a packet of food or different fruit and then the first person who shouted out where it came from was given it as a prize. I was good at Geography so I did quite well, but I felt sorry that the people who really could do with the extra foodstuff didn't know the country of origin or they were too slow. This early Socialist trend did not prevent me from putting all my energies into shouting out first. Finally we all repaired to the field below the gardens and ran races: potato sack, egg and spoon, all for prizes of chocolates.

St Giles' Fair

We would never miss St. Giles' Fair, which was always held during the first Monday and Tuesday of September. Mother took us by carrier's cart, but most of the village children and their mothers walked over the fields to 'Mesopotamia' in North Oxford. The Warner family had two in the pram and three walking and they stayed all day, but were only allowed one ride. Did managed to get lost and was taken crying to the lost children's centre when she suddenly saw the pattern on her mother's skirt and realised that she was being rescued.

St Giles' Fair, 1908. © Oxfordshire County Council Photographic Archive.

To me the fair was complete magic: especially the galloping horses with their graceful movement, rising and falling, as they swept majestically round. Many of the rides would be considered too tame for the children of today, such as the leisurely swing boats, but at least we worked them ourselves, pulling on the colourful, fuzzy ropes. We disdained the juddering cakewalk, which was more for our mothers' generation.

I wanted to go on the chair-a-plane, where you sat on a seat hung by a long chair and went whizzing round at a break-neck pace, but mother said no – a child had got killed in one. I thought that I bet he didn't do up his seat belt. Later there was a big wheel and we queued up for it, but our courage deserted us at the last minute. We consoled ourselves at the fish and chip stall and the penny bazaar where we bought trinkets and peg-dolls.

Nowadays many of these 'rides' are obsolete and have been relegated to museum status. In Norfolk they have the old-fashioned steam engines, also a sort of switchback going up and down like the galloping horses, but also round and round at the same time, and there is only one left that is working.

Bonfire Night

The Watts's bonfire night was always a great occasion and the enormous bonfire was prepared days ahead with faggots, brushwood and logs, piled as high as a house on the hill overlooking Oxford. We all brought our own modest collections of fireworks: coloured matches at ½d a box, Catherine wheels, squibs ½d, ½d jumping jacks and sparklers. The more affluent provided roman candles and rockets.

Our own firework party on the next night was less spectacular in our little backyard, but we did have a splendid box of Paynes's Assorted Fireworks and we provided potatoes baked in their jackets. The Buchan family joined in the festivities like the rest of the village children; Alistair Buchan chose a 'Fiery Serpent' cracker from the box; it took a long time to get active and his aristocratic voice was heard, "But where are the fiery serpents?" and the next minute he was jumping all over the place with the fiery serpents pursuing him!

There were also a number of very minor celebrations, which were beginning to go into decline.

Valentine's Day. At one time, before mine, children would go from door to door singing, "Please to give us a Valentine; I'll be yours if you'll be mine." It was a ritual for collecting a few sweets and this usually reached its climax outside the village shop, when the owner was duty bound to throw nuts, sweets and apples to the crowd of children, which had assembled.

Pancake Day was widely celebrated and apart from having once-a-year pancakes for dinner, there used to be a Pancake race, down the village road with the competitors racing with a pancake in a frying pan, which they tossed as they ran.

Mother's Day was far removed from the commercialised version of today. It was always called Mothering Sunday, and originated in the custom of allowing girls in service to bake a cake and take it to their mothers once a year. They often had to walk miles to reach their homes – and get back the same day.

My own holiday. After a bout of measles, chicken pox, jaundice and pneumonia, it was decided that I needed sea air, and Auntie Lucy took me to join Auntie Edie and Uncle Jack at Cliftonville. In the photograph below, I am front right with Auntie Edie behind me. Uncle Jack is behind her to the left.

Appendix

A Potted History of Elsfield

People have lived at Elsfield since the Bronze Age and probably much earlier, as it is a strategic site being perched on a hill overlooking the City of Oxford. There were probably Roman settlers, as Roman remains have been found nearby. The name, Elsfield, means the field of an Anglo-Saxon, called Ella or Elesa.

When the Domesday Book was compiled in 1086, Elsfield was entered as part of the whole possessions of the Norman, Robert d'Oilley, who built Oxford Castle. Five-eights of the arable land, between 80 and 144 acres belonged to his desmesne, the land from which he took the produce. The work of the desmesne was done by the tenants of the remaining three eights, which meant that they had to work for the majority of the time for the lord of the Manor.

There were two classes of tenants: eleven substantial men called villeins, which originally meant villagers, and seven lesser men called borders or cottagers. Five slaves were also recorded and six other men. Besides his share of the arable land, each tenant had his rights of common, such as the right to turn out a fixed number of beasts to graze and to take a fixed share of hay from the common meadows. Most of the work was jointly organised and carried out, but the animals, the corn and the hay belonged to individual owners, from the lord down to the borders. With women and children the whole population may have numbered about a hundred. In addition to their labour, the Tenants collectively owed the lord thirteen baskets of nuts each year.

Elsfield was surrounded by forests, which from William the Conqueror onwards was designated land, preventing all unauthorised persons from hunting deer or cutting down timber. Later Elsfield and certain other villages had the right of allowing their pigs in the forest taken away and they had to pay for the privilege at the rate of so much for every eight pigs.

The next source of information about the village was entitled the Hundred Rolls, which gave a much fuller picture than the Domesday Book. By that time, the arable, pasture and meadow land had greatly increased, owing to the clearing of some of the forest land, which to this day surrounds much of Elsfield. There were no longer any slaves. There were only eight tenants in place of the eleven villeins and the cottagers had increased to twenty-four. A few of the villagers were mentioned by name, which indicates that to some extent their occupations were specialised, for example; Henry the Smith, Richard the Woodward, Robert the Cooper and William the Miller.

The mill at Sescut, on the Cherwell, may have been there from very early times and the village boundary makes a detour to include it and the adjoining meadow. The tenants all had to bring their corn to be ground, with the miller taking his share as payment. The lord had a right of corn milling, which was only gradually abolished by the sixteenth century, as was his sole right to keep pigeons until then, which meant that the villagers were deprived of a food source and also valuable manure.

By the time of the Hundred Rolls, the tenants and cottagers alike all either worked for the lord of the Manor or paid rent or a mixture of the two. Paying rent, they would have more time to spend on their strips of land, but it could be hard to find the money to pay. Their holdings were often measured in strips in open fields and apparently the number of strips gradually increased to each tenant from two to four over the centuries. They were hard done by with regard to their rights of grazing on the common land and taking a portion of hay mown from the common meadows, when the laws of the enclosures were given to the lord or his friends.

The next most powerful influence after the manor was the church and Elsfield church was established in the early part of the thirteenth century and the vicar was to receive five-eights of the whole value of the church. This was calculated on the basis of the offerings or collections made at the services, tithes of corn and hay and small tithes, an acre of land and the vicarage. After some years, as a result of a run of bad harvests, the vicar's emolument was no longer sufficient and the canons of the church decided to give him three quarters of corn a year, which was later continued in the form of money payment. This seems to have been a generous allowance.

St Frideswide's rectors were entitled to some of the tithes and were also granted more land in the village; for example, Hugh of Elsfield gave four acres as a penance for his unfaithful payment of tithes. Later, Simon of Elsfield, the then lard of the Manor, granted all his property in Elsfield, namely a fifth part of the Manor with all its appurtenant common rights and dues. For this he was to receive something in return: sums of money for himself and his wife, a palfrey for his son and a corrody for himself or his son, whichever should be the survivor. Apparently a corrody (pension) meant to be supported for life at St. Frideswide's on the same scale of living as a canon and this seemed to be an excellent way of providing for old age. Later, Thomas of Elsfield made an exchange with the canons of St. Frideswide, by which he gave them 74 acres of arable land with wood, meadow and pasture from his demesne and they surrendered to him their fifth part of the Manor. The canons had a grange or messuage to store the produce of their land and tithes, with a dwelling place for their man in charge. So there were a lot of transactions between the Manor and the church, which the villagers had no inkling of, although their rent and labour helped to pay for the moneys that were exchanged.

The sixteenth century saw many innovations. Elsfield was affected by the religious changes when the services, the vestments and the ornaments were altered in accordance with the decisions and counter-decisions of sovereigns and parliaments. With the dissolution of the monasteries, St. Frideswide's ceased to exist. The rectory came into the hands of the lord of the Manor, whose successors have held it ever since. Finally, by the middle of the seventeenth century, a family called Pudsey gradually bought all the property, including St. Frideswide's, to make them proprietors of the whole Elsfield parish of 1,200 acres, with the exception of the glebe land.

There is much less information about the villagers, whose lives were heavily burdened with endless toil and struggle against poverty. A rare report of a conspiracy, led by humble folk with grievances against the practice of enclosures, which denied the poor their rights to graze their livestock on common land, is described as a feeble attempt at a rising against Queen Elizabeth's government. Elsfield was evidently involved, as George Pudsey, the then squire, was accused of offering to be their leader; but although the lord lieutenant was ordered to arrest him, no more is known, so probably the matter ended there.

Towards the end of the seventeenth century, the estate was in difficulties and the then lord, Thomas Pudsey, had to sell it to Lord North, later created Earl of Guildford. The Norths were absentee landlords and in fact the son was prime minister for twelve years. They were drawing about £1,500 a year from Elsfield in rents, which was a huge sum in those days. It was not surprising that, towards the end of the eighteenth century, Elsfield was described as a village with a great appearance of poverty and the villagers were hard put to make ends meet. The women managed to earn some money by spinning and by the mid-nineteenth century the census reported eight people who did not work on the land: a mason, two sawyers, a cabinet-maker, a laundress, a shopkeeper and a fruit dealer.

By the end of the nineteenth century, the full force of the agricultural depression was felt. A banker, Mr Herbert Parsons, then bought the whole of the Elsfield estate from Lord North and kept it until 1919 when Christ

Church College, Oxford, bought it, taking over a large part of the possessions of St. Frideswide's. Whoever owned the estate, the management was minimal, only a few cottages built and no other building or development. Fortunately for the village, Christ Church sold the Manor House to John Buchan, the well-known author and, later, Governor of Canada. He and his family played a very active part in the village life and this was altogether new, as although the Parsons family participated in the village, theirs was a much more authoritarian regime, tempered with benevolence.

From the early part of the twentieth century onwards, changes were taking place and mechanisation was beginning to lessen the need for agricultural workers and some cottagers found employment in the new industries in Oxford. But Elsfield still flourished with dairy cattle and Oxford Down sheep, so there was no organic change until the Second World War. Scientific farming reduced still further the need for workers in the nineteen fifties onwards and the cottages, previously tied to the job on the farm, were beginning to be sold off, although Christ Church College kept the farms for rental.

In the fifties, the school, which had been in existence for over one hundred years, finally closed down, as did the village shop and Post Office, and a few years later the building was demolished. So now Elsfield is a very different place, with a preponderance of middle class inhabitants and the remaining farm workers in old people's homes in neighbouring Marston. The church still has services, but the vicar has three parishes to care for: Beckley, Horton cum Studley and Elsfield.

I should like to pay special tribute to Sir George Clark, whose pamphlet written in 1975 has provided me with most of the information contained in this brief summary. His work, entitled 'Elsfield, Church and Village', deserves to be more widely known. Published by the author in 1975, it is available from Christ Church, Oxford.